STRONGER MAN NATION
Biblical Manhood Series

SOLDIER
BUILT TO PROTECT

Adam James

SOLDIER: Built To Protect

Copyright © 2022

Scriptures taken from the Holy Bible, New International Version®, NIV®. Copyright © 1973, 1978, 1984, 2011 by Biblica, Inc.™ Used by permission of Zondervan. All rights reserved worldwide. www.zondervan.com The "NIV" and "New International Version"are trademarks registered in the United States Patent and Trademark Office by Biblica, Inc.™

Published by Grace City Publishing

All rights reserved. No part of this publication may be reproduced in any form, stored in a retrieval system, or transmitted in any form by any means—electronic, mechanical, photocopy, recording, or otherwise—without the prior permission of the publisher, except as provided by United States of America copyright law.

Editorial Team: Luke Ellington, Chief Editor; Karis McPherson, Art Director; and the Proofreading Team.

Printed in the United States of America.

To my sons, Benjamin and Samuel, who I love with my whole heart.

To my fellow elders—you're the men I call first.

To the Stronger Men of Grace City Church. It's my privilege and joy to be among you.

You then, my **SON**, be strong in the grace that is in Christ Jesus. And the things you have heard me say in the presence of many witnesses entrust to reliable men who will also be qualified to teach others. Join with me in suffering, like a good **SOLDIER** of Christ Jesus. No one serving as a soldier gets entangled in civilian affairs, but rather tries to please his commanding officer. Similarly, anyone who competes as an **ATHLETE** does not receive the victor's crown except by competing according to the rules. The hardworking **FARMER** should be the first to receive a share of the crops. Reflect on what I am saying, for the Lord will give you insight into all this.

2 TIMOTHY 2:1-7

STRONGER MAN NATION

is a movement of like-minded men.

We're living out biblical manhood
with clear eyes in a confused culture.

We're committed to making good battle
with our lives. We follow the Stronger Man
— Jesus Christ —
and we'd love for you to join us.

→ Annual conference on Father's Day weekend.

→ Monthly rallies.

→ Project ManCard Rite-of-Passage Experiences for fathers and sons.

→ Helpful resources.

WWW.STRONGERMANNATION.COM

CONTENTS

Acknowledgments 1

Foreword 3

Introduction 7

WEEK 1 STRONGER MEN LIVE LIKE GOOD SOLDIERS (2 Timothy 2:3-4) 10

WEEK 2 KNOW YOUR ENEMY AND WALK IN VICTORY (Rev. 12:7-12) 20

WEEK 3 EQUIPPED FOR BATTLE (Ephesians 6:10-20) 32

WEEK 4 TAKE EVERY THOUGHT CAPTIVE (2 Corinthians 10:3-5) 42

WEEK 5 ACT LIKE MEN (1 Corinthians 16:13-14) 54

WEEK 6 HUMBLE, ALERT, SOBER (1 Peter 5:5-11) 64

WEEK 7 UNDERSTAND AUTHORITY, FAITH, & OBEDIENCE (Matt. 8:5-13) 74

WEEK 8 WHEN STRONGER MEN DON'T GO OUT TO WAR (2 Sam. 11:1-4) 84

WEEK 9 PRAY TO GOD AND POST A GUARD (Nehemiah 4:7-9,13-14) 94

WEEK 10 THE WORLD IS NOT WORTHY (Hebrews 11:32-38) 104

WEEK 11 STRONGER MEN MAKE STRONGER MEN (Matthew 28:18-20) 114

WEEK 12 THE STRONGER MAN WILL FINISH THE WAR (Revelation 19:11-16)...126

Additional Questions For Discussion 136

Practical Ways To Lean Into Being A Soldier, Built To Protect 138

The Stronger Man Creed 140

ACKNOWLEDGMENTS

To Pastor Josh McPherson, my friend and the best leader I know, thank you for leading the way and letting me come along. To my Uncle Bruce and Aunt Lorrie, for providing a place to pray and write. To the people who prayed...Dad, Mom, Greg, Steve, Jeff, Ted, AR, Sam, and others—thank you. To the incredibly gifted Luke and Karis, for your work to edit, design layout, and bring this into existence. To the faithful Stronger Men who contributed testimonies and words of exhortation, thank you. To my wife, Erin, my greatest encourager and supporter, thank you for your steadfast belief, for being with me on the retreats, and for your editing eye. And to my girls, Grace and Noelle, you make me a better dad and man.

FOREWORD

Welcome to Stronger Man Nation. A way of life for the bold.

The book you are holding will make you a Stronger Man.

I say this with great confidence, mainly because the man who wrote it has pushed me to be a Stronger Man for twenty-five years.

I first met Adam in college. I was a straitlaced, homeschooled kid naive to the ways of the world, Adam a swaggering punk on the basketball team living for the next big party. Not a likely pair.

But Jesus is in the habit of converging the roads of unlikely friends and forging between them deep bonds of camaraderie and brotherhood. And so He did.

Since then, we've spent the better part of a quarter century shoulder-to-shoulder in the trenches working, sweating, dreaming, laughing, and all-around making merry battle on the fields of full-time ministry. It has been, for me, a life-changing friendship.

I say life-changing because when you get anywhere near the Adam James orbit, you encounter a white-hot nuclear reactor pulsing with spiritual passion. Adam's affection for Jesus is contagious. If you don't have a fire for Jesus, he'll start one. If you've got one, he'll stoke it hot. It's just the James way.

Which is why, one cold, winter afternoon, I walked out to his job trailer with an idea for the men of our church. I wanted Adam to crack the door of his soul-furnace and expose them to the blast of heat that emanates from a heart on fire for God's glory.

When I asked him if he would write a resource for men built around the four cornerstone identities of Stronger Man Nation, it was not only because I thought him a good writer, which he is. I asked him because Adam is a good man. And more importantly, he's good at being a man.

And we desperately need more good men good at being men.

Why? Well, allow me to speak plainly. The days are evil, men are wimps, and the enemy is playing for keeps.

Let's break that down.

The days are evil. As I write, it's legal in my town for the state to shuttle a child to a "gender therapy" center and begin irreversible hormonal castration or surgical mutilation (whichever the 14-year-old and their state-assigned counselor deem most beneficial for the child's mental health).

And all of this can be done without a parent's knowledge or permission.

But that same kid couldn't go to a tanning salon without parental consent, because the same state that hides gender reassignment "therapy" from parents has deemed getting a tan potentially too harmful for a child's health to attempt without parental permission.

As you can see, not only are the days abhorrently evil, they are absurdly bizarre.

Men are wimps. Okay, let me qualify that. Not every man is a wimp. Just too many of them. The masculinity crisis of our day is well documented. Men are on the run, chased into the shadows by a cancel culture built to swarm any man who dares show a hint of brawny moral backbone.

It's not so much that men have lost their way—they have lost their proverbial nerve. It's not that being a Stronger Man is a mystery, it's that being a Stronger Man takes guts. And guts, these days, are in short supply.

Thankfully, this is not true of the men and sons who make up Stronger Man Nation. May their tribe increase.

The enemy is playing for keeps. Here's some more plain speak...the enemy has your number and he's coming for you full throttle. War is upon us and the bullets are real. The cost for a lack of vigilance is steep. The enemy has breached the gate.

It's time that we, as Christian men, circle the wagons, grow a pair, and mount a counter-offensive. It's time we stop looking for the path of least resistance and start picking the biggest enemy target we can find and charging it with a whoop and a holler.

It's time we flip the script. No longer is the enemy hunting us—we are hunting him. And we have a bone to pick. "The gates of Hell will not prevail..." assumes an offensive posture of God's men. It's time to live like it.

If any of that resonates in your heart, this devotional book is for you. It will help you become that kind of man—a man who learns how to submit to the Lordship of Jesus Christ, and in so doing, becomes dangerous to the kingdom of darkness.

I am deeply grateful that these original devotionals, which Adam wrote for the men of our house, are now being made available to a wider audience in this power-packed, four-part series. I have witnessed, firsthand, the fire it has stoked in hundreds and hundreds of men in our local church. I pray it does the same for you.

God is writing a divine story of glory for your life. Don't miss it. The pages of these books will help you see that story, and more importantly, show you how to step into it with gumption. This isn't just a book to read; it's a playbook to live. There is an immediacy to its application. It's a field guide for how to start being a Stronger Man today.

However this book got into your hands, consider it the grace of God. He must love you (maybe more than you thought) and have good battle for you to make in the days and weeks ahead. Thrilling.

So grab some dudes, get a time on the calendar, and get after it. Time is ticking, the war is raging, and we need more fierce warriors happily slaying dragons with zeal and prejudice.

I look forward to seeing you on the field of battle.

Pastor Josh McPherson
Founder, Stronger Man Nation
Lead Pastor, Grace City Church

INTRODUCTION

As I write this, I'm sitting at the desk of a former Brigadier General in the United States Air Force. Plaques and awards cover the walls. His flight suit hangs in the closet. And his desk is the way he left it before he passed.

There's something about a long and distinguished military career that exudes admirable qualities of honor, duty, service, and protection. It feels manly. It feels good and right. Those feelings speak to the reality that hardwired into men is the design and desire to serve a higher purpose and protect those we love. Those aren't the only qualities required for noble manhood, but they're certainly a critical part of it.

I often wish I had served in the Armed Forces. The closest I've ever come to actual physical war is pretending as a young boy and a few fistfights growing up.

My dad was in the Army reserves for a short time after college. My two brothers and I grew up pretending to be soldiers as we dressed up in his old fatigues and headed out into the hills behind my small-town Eastern Washington home with MREs for a day of imaginary warfare with our BB guns or homemade rubber band guns (this was before Airsoft existed).

I've known many friends and acquaintances who have served in the Armed Forces, and if that's you reading this—I salute you. I honor your service and sacrifice. I will never not say "thank you for your service" to those I meet who have served in any role, in any branch, of our nation's military. It is worthy of honor and respect.

This book is not written to train physical soldiers. This book is written to encourage and equip you to be a spiritual soldier—a Stronger Man of God. The Bible itself tells us that mature and honorable manhood is like being a good soldier in some very important and profound ways.

As soldiers, God made men to be protectors. He made men for a mission. Men are called to exercise the ability and strength to endure hardship, to focus on the mission, to avoid life-threatening distractions and entanglements, and to ultimately aim to please their commanding officer—the Lord Jesus Christ.

While we may not all experience physical combat or serve in the Armed Forces, the reality is we were all born into a war. Since the beginning, there has been a spiritual war going on for the hearts, minds, and souls of men.

All men are called to be like soldiers—ready, willing, and able to put themselves in harm's way to protect women, children and the weak and vulnerable.

The Apostle Paul wrote his final letter, his second letter to his spiritual son and pastoral protégé, Timothy, to pass the baton of the mission of God to the next generation of men. They would, in turn, pass it on to the next generation. And those men to the next.

He wanted Timothy and those men who would follow to think of themselves and conduct themselves in 4 distinct ways: like good soldiers, athletes, farmers, and sons. These four images, right from the pages of Scripture in 2 Timothy chapter 2, carry much of the essence of true and noble manhood.

At the center of Paul's strategy, the Bible's strategy (aka God's strategy), is raising up more men. Stronger Men. Strong in the grace of God. The call was for Timothy himself to *become* a stronger, godly man and to pass on what he had been given to *build* up another generation of godly, Stronger Men. Who will, in turn, love, lead, and *bless* women and children and the Church as well.

Become. Build. Bless. That's the three-pronged, singular call of God for men. Become Stronger Men who build Stronger Men who bless women, children, the Church, and world.

God's great mission, the redemption and salvation of the world, requires a man-making mission.

All through the Scriptures and the story of God, men are called to be protectors, providers, leaders, and lovers. These roles are seen in the four images of the soldier, farmer, athlete and son.

In these 4 images there is a mountain of manhood to be explored. There is a lifetime of growth and maturity and responsibility to receive. These masculine images have carried the ethos of true manhood for millennia.

They are not four different men. They are to be woven into one image—four parts of one man—who finds his ultimate model and perfect example in the person of Jesus Christ.

These four man-types are a picture of the divine design of noble manhood, and they come with a living promise in 2 Timothy—*"Reflect on what I am saying, for the Lord will give you insight into all this."*

And we'd be wise to reflect on them afresh and rediscover those spiritual insights today.

The need arises in every generation. The battle is raging again as intense as ever before. It's our turn to answer the call.

God has given us a blueprint for the task. Let's dig in!

WEEK 1

STRONGER MEN LIVE LIKE GOOD SOLDIERS

> Join with me in suffering, like a good **SOLDIER** of Christ Jesus. No one serving as a soldier gets entangled in civilian affairs, but rather tries to please his commanding officer.
>
> **2 TIMOTHY 2:3-4**

SOLDIER

Manhood, like being a good soldier, is not for the faint of heart.

If you set out to become a Stronger Man, which you should, know there will be resistance. There will be opposition. You will experience various forms and degrees of attack and suffering.

In his final instruction to Timothy—after charging him with the task of entrusting the gospel to reliable men who will in turn pass it on to others (2 Timothy 2:2)—the Apostle Paul issues a call to suffer in the sacrificial service of God's mission and purposes.

"Join with me in suffering."

"Endure suffering."

Paul understood the realities of conflict. He was writing from prison. He understood the consequences of spiritual war. He viewed the entire Christian life as "fighting the good fight," and he knew he was nearing the end of his.

WEEK ONE

He paid the price many times over through his own persecution, harassment, abandonment, beatings, imprisonment, false accusations, character assassinations, and eventual death.

Cancel culture would have had a field day with Paul. But it would have been a cakewalk compared to what he actually endured. And Paul would have stood his ground, fearlessly spoken truth, and kept fighting the good fight.

He knew the path of suffering, and he didn't shrink back. He issued that same call to Timothy, and he issues it to you and me.

To all men reading this: it's time to enlist.

In spite of the continued cultural collapse in Western society, especially in matters of gender, sexuality, masculinity and femininity, the Bible's call to men has not evolved or progressed. The biological and binary divine design of truth about men and women resonates in every generation. But it's under attack. Manhood is not for the faint of heart.

Manhood requires deep conviction and stouthearted perseverance. You have to actually BELIEVE. Becoming a Stronger Man who is living out God's mission isn't just "part" of your life—it's the overarching PURPOSE for your life.

It's got to be in your bones.

If it's not, you simply won't stand up to the attacks. You won't hold the line.

So let me ask, do you have a strong desire to live out God's purpose for your life? For a mission big enough to live and die for?

Stronger Men tap into that desire and calling, fan it into flame, and respond with a deep "yes." And that comes with a cost.

That mission starts in your heart, flows through your home, then into your world. It encompasses every relationship and every endeavor in your life.

Manhood, like being a good soldier, is relentlessly bombarded with distractions and deadly entanglements.

Good soldiers don't get entangled in civilian affairs. To the degree that you are ordering your life around the mission of God, anything short of sin can be utilized and leveraged for the right mission.

Anything, even good things, maybe *especially* good things, can also be massive distractions and suck the time, energy, money, and passion of men away from the things of God.

How many men end up "entangled?" Whether through blatant sin, seductive mediocrity, deadly lethargy, classic excuse-making, or chasing the things of this world...the side of the road is littered with the bones of men who got caught in the barbed wire.

If you're entangled as you read this, you need to know that there is help and there is hope. It's time to speak up, own up, admit it, and get around men who are running after God.

We all feel the pull of the enemy. Around us and within us. You're not alone. But as a man, with the help of the Holy Spirit, you can resist. You must.

Men are built to pursue something. To attack it, defeat it, conquer it. The only question is, are you pursuing the right things? Are you on the right mission? Or are you getting entangled in "civilian affairs?" Are you just running the same race as the culture around you?

You don't have any more time to waste. It's time to focus on the only mission that counts.

Stronger Men, like good soldiers, have the ultimate aim of pleasing their commanding officer.

There's only One worthy of aiming to please: the Stronger Man, Jesus Christ.

You, brother, will continuously be bombarded. Have you noticed? You'll take some punches. You won't be perfect. But you've got to keep trying. And just so I'm not misunderstood, your "trying" isn't you pulling yourself up by your own bootstraps. This isn't macho masculinity. This is humble, honest, earnest desire to follow Jesus and live for Him above all. To do that, you've got to depend on His grace and His strength to help keep you from getting entangled, staying entangled, or going the wrong way.

"Trying" is less about your *strength* and more about your *aim*.

What are you aiming at? If your life is like a gun with a scope...what do you see when you look through the scope? What are you aiming at? What's in the bullseye? If someone were to hang out with you, follow you around for a month, listen in on your conversations, see how you spend your money and time...what would they say you're aiming at?

WEEK ONE

A Stronger Man is aiming at a life that pleases and glorifies God above all else. His life, his marriage, his family, his business, his resources, his influence, his opportunities, his witness, his character, his reputation, his passions, his impact, and his legacy. All of it, all of life, is being considered through that lens. All of life is being leveraged to that end.

Jesus is always our ultimate example. He set His face like a flint toward Jerusalem. Resolute. Focused. Even as a 12-year-old boy, He was already resolved and devoted to His Heavenly Father's will and plans for His life. Jesus fixed His eyes on His Father and ruthlessly focused on His mission. He fixed His eyes on the cross. He called people to follow Him and at times He ticked off crowds. He wasn't living to please the masses. He knew when to move on and He knew when to invest more, whether those He was healing and serving or those He was equipping and training. He embraced suffering, resisted temptation and entanglements, even when physically exhausted and depleted, and finished the race with His righteousness intact. And He did it so that He could be the all-sufficient Savior that you and I need. He's not just our example, He's the source of the actual transforming grace and power we need to become like Him. He lived to please His Father. He endured to the end—drilled the bullseye—so that in turn He could empower us by His grace and His Spirit to walk in His footsteps. Let's keep looking to Him.

LET'S PRAY

Father, keep me focused on You today. Thank You for my life, my family, my job, my church family...all of it is from You and for You. Guide me today. Show me where You are at work in those around me. Help me give my best, do my best, and someway, somehow point people to You. Give me the courage to stand for truth and to do so in a wise, unapologetic, and godly manner. Thank You for forgiving me, helping me, and strengthening me to live for You. In Jesus' Name, amen.

SOLDIER

FROM A STRONGER MAN

There is an old saying, "there are no atheists in a fox hole." It is likely true that many individuals who have not come to call on God for a personal relationship before, do so when under intense fire from the enemy. The unconverted at this point are faced with all their human fears and fragility in one moment. However, the seasoned believer at their side, while experiencing some natural fear, is simultaneously secure in the steadfast hope that God has ordained their days, and that they can truly experience the peace that passes all understanding amidst conflict.

The disposition of the man of God in this scenario is not developed in 6 weeks at basic training. It is rooted in years of understanding that we are called into a relationship with God where scripture is replete with examples that the Christian walk is a daily struggle. It is a war where some enemies are seen, others are not, but one constant remains: **We must dress for battle daily and be alert at all times** with our weapons of spiritual warfare trained and sharpened so that when confronted by assault or temptation we remain strong and grounded. We must be ready in advance of attacks so that we can act and make decisions for the Kingdom while under fire.

Dave, 62

WEEK ONE

> "So let us understand the situation. We are goin' into battle against a tough and determined enemy. I can't promise you that I will bring you all home alive. But this I swear before you and before Almighty God: That when we go into battle, I will be the first to set foot on the field, and I will be the last to step off. And I will leave no one behind. Dead or alive, we will all come home together. So help me God."
>
> — Col. Hal Moore (Mel Gibson, *We Were Soldiers*)

SOLDIER

REFLECT & DISCUSS

1. In what ways do you recognize spiritual resistance and opposition?

_____
_____
_____

2. Where are you in danger of being (or actually currently) "entangled?" What is the number one threat to your ability to stay focused on the mission? And what's one thing you can do this week to eliminate that deadly distraction?

_____
_____
_____

3. How's your current aim? If someone followed you around for a month, what kinds of things would they say your life is aiming at?

_____
_____
_____

4. What kind of filter do you use when making a commitment with your time, energy, or resources?

_____
_____
_____

5. When you think about the possibility of suffering for your faith, what comes to mind? How do you think/feel about that prospect?

___

6. How can you prepare yourself and your family now to be able to endure potential suffering for your faith?

___

7. How can you, in a practical way, throughout the course of any given period of time (day, week, month, quarter, year), sharpen and maintain your aim on pleasing God?

___

TAKE ACTION

- Memorize 2 Timothy 2:3-4.

- Finish this sentence: The main purpose of my life is...

- Evaluate your current commitments: relationships, work, school, job, sports, travel, extra-curricular, church, etc. Is there a clear purpose for each commitment? Are any of your commitments taking you away from a life focused on God's purposes and mission for your life? Are any of your commitments taking you away from church and a commitment to participation with the mission and ministry of God's people?

- How are you leveraging these commitments for your growth, the spiritual growth of your family, and spiritual impact on those around you?

WEEK 2

KNOW YOUR ENEMY AND WALK IN VICTORY

Then war broke out in Heaven. Michael and his angels fought against the dragon, and the dragon and his angels fought back. But he was not strong enough, and they lost their place in Heaven. The great dragon was hurled down—that ancient serpent called the devil, or Satan, who leads the whole world astray. He was hurled to the earth, and his angels with him.

Then I heard a loud voice in Heaven say:
"Now have come the salvation and the power
   and the Kingdom of our God,
     and the authority of His Messiah.
For the accuser of our brothers and sisters,
   who accuses them before our God day and night, has been hurled down.

They triumphed over him by the blood of the Lamb

   and by the word of their testimony;
they did not love their lives so much
   as to shrink from death.

Therefore rejoice, you heavens
   and you who dwell in them!
But woe to the earth and the sea,
   because the devil has gone down to you!
He is filled with fury,
   because he knows that his time is short."

REVELATION 12:7-12

A good soldier knows about his enemy—his tactics, his nature, his capabilities.

There are a few basic things we need to know about Satan. Not because we want to fixate or become consumed with thinking about our enemy but because the Bible says we are not "*unaware of the devil's schemes*" (**2 Corinthians 2:11**).

While not exhaustive, Revelation 12 is a helpful text to that end. You'll notice in this passage, we learn that war broke out in Heaven and spilled over into the earth.

Congratulations, you've been caught in the crossfire. And you're actually in the crosshairs. It's a real war that started before you and is still raging today. Like it or not, war is upon you. Think "Lord of the Rings." Think "The Patriot." There's no avoiding it.

The enemy is on your doorstep. He's crouching at your door (Genesis 4:7). He wants to burn your house down.

What do we learn about our enemy, the devil, in this passage?

→ **He's a hater and a fighter. He started a riot in Heaven. Let's just say it: Satan is a punk.**

→ **He's a loser. He lost the battle in Heaven. He got kicked out.**

→ **He's weaker than God's angels. Notice he's not an equal and opposite of God. He fought other angels and lost. Keep that in mind. Whose side do you want to be on?**

→ **He's a deceiver and is cunning enough to deceive the world and lead the world astray. Read Ephesians 2:1-3.**

→ **He's a leader. He leads the wrong team. In the wrong direction.**

→ **He's an accuser. Unfortunately, with a lot of energy (he accuses day and night).**

→ **He's a loser on earth. True believers triumph over him. Keep that in mind. And note in the text how we gain victory!**

→ **He and his demons (evil angels) make life harder. He adds to the pain, suffering, and trouble we experience in this life. It is dangerous down here.**

→ **He's angry (filled with fury) because he knows his time is short.**

Additionally, you'll notice he's called the great dragon. One way to summarize the entire story of the Bible, the journey of the Christian life, and the life of men is this:

KILL THE DRAGON, WIN THE GIRL.

It's the ethos and motto of Stronger Man Nation. "Kill the dragon, Win the girl."

It's what Jesus has done, is doing, and will ultimately do. He defeats Satan and wins His Bride (the Church).

It's what men are called to do in Jesus' Name, as well.

How do we kill the dragon? How do we triumph in this spiritual battle?

"They triumphed over him by the blood of the Lamb and by the word of their testimony; they did not love their lives so much as to shrink from death."

Our victory is found in the cross of Jesus Christ, the Lamb of God. Through true repentance, genuine faith, and the power of the Holy Spirit, we are empowered to persevere and endure to the end, even if it costs us our very lives.

The cross is where the accusations of the enemy are defeated and silenced (Colossians 2:13-15).

The "word of their testimony" encompasses both the Word of God (the testimony of His prophets and apostles) and the testimony of true, born-again followers of Jesus who can say (and bear the fruit of), *"Jesus is Lord, and He is my Lord. He is my Savior, and I belong to Him. I am a redeemed child of God. My sin has been forgiven, my debt paid, my judgment absorbed and I am clothed in the righteousness of Jesus."*

I was blind, but now I see.
I was dead, but now I am alive.
I was lost, but now am found.

I was in chains, but now I'm free. The old is gone, the new has come.

Is that your story? Is that your testimony? Has your life been changed by the grace, truth, and power of Jesus? Can you talk about it with passion in your heart and fire in your eyes?

Those who overcome the enemy are those who persevere IN faith, BY faith, to the end.

Jesus said, "What does it profit a man to gain the world but lose his soul?" And, "if you seek to save your life you will lose it." And, "if you deny me before men I will deny you before my Father in Heaven."

Men are still tempted to seek self-centered comfort more than courageous conviction. Stronger Men slay that dragon. Again and again.

These issues and line-in-the-sand questions take us to the bottom line. Who or what is your highest priority and allegiance. Jesus? Or Self?

How much do you love your life? The question does not assume you should hate your life. I have a great life. Filled with amazing blessings and relationships. But if push came to shove, I wouldn't deny Jesus to try to cling to my life as though this life and this world is all I have or all there is.

That hasn't always been the case. As a younger man, I totally sold out Jesus for the world and its offer to me of a "fun" life. I wanted certain people to like me more than I wanted to please God. The reality is, I didn't actually know God. Once I got to know Him, that all changed.

Have you counted the cost of truly following Jesus? How will you not waver when put to the test?

When accused by the enemy, when filled with fear or doubt, what is the anchor of your confidence that keeps you from drifting or crashing? What is your strategy for engaging and overcoming with overwhelming spiritual firepower?

Stronger Men know how to wield the power of the cross. They know the power of the blood of Jesus, the substitutionary atonement that is at the heart of the gospel message. And against which, no devil or demon can stand. They know the power of the testimony of God's Word and the faith that believes God even in the midst of overwhelming pressure. And they have thought through their ultimate priorities. They've run the drill and they are resolved to lay it all on the line, leave it all on the field, and stand their ground, come hell or high water.

Are you currently taking these spiritual realities seriously? Are you focused and aware? Staying vigilant? In the fight?

WEEK TWO

You can be that kind of man. I believe you're reading this because you are that kind of man.

And if you are reading this and know you've failed to hold the line... there's still hope.

There may well be consequences that roll out, but with Jesus, there's always hope and there's always help. No matter how steep the climb or tough the fight, the truth remains for those who belong to Jesus: "*Greater is He who is in you than he who is in the world*" (**1 John 4:4**).

So get up and keep fighting. Turn to Jesus in repentance, own your sin and shortcoming, and get your strength back at the foot of the cross.

Satan will try and accuse you and get you to give up. His time is short, but your future is secure. Remember, if you're in Christ, you're on the winning side.

LET'S PRAY

Father, thank You for the victory of the cross! Thank You, Jesus, for laying down Your life and defeating Satan on my behalf. Thank You for kicking him out of Heaven. Now help me join the battle on earth and keep handing him more defeats in my life and the lives of those in my life through the blood of Jesus. Thank You for the saving power and authority of Jesus. In Jesus' Name, amen.

WEEK TWO

> "No matter how much it hurts,
> how dark it gets or
> no matter how far you fall.
> You are never out of the fight."
>
> — Marcus Luttrell, Lone Survivor

SOLDIER

A Personal Story

Did you know Satan can actually end up unwittingly being an evangelist and leading people to Jesus? That's not his aim, but that's the wisdom and power of our God. To take what the enemy intends for evil and to use it as His means of turning the tide in His direction. It's what happened at the cross. Satan's greatest victory became his ultimate defeat.

Even when Satan gets a shot off, he often shoots himself in the foot. No wonder he's so angry.

I had been raised in the Church. I learned the Bible stories and was taught about Jesus. But I chose the world. I wanted the approval of others. I wanted to call my own shots. I believed the lies and walked in darkness instead of light. When I got to college, it only got worse. Then an old friend invited me to a Bible study for college age kids. She asked me if I still believed in God. "Of course!" I said. But inwardly, I had doubts. Was God even real? And if He was, surely I was just doing what every normal college kid does, I thought...having fun, partying, being in college.

I finally decided to go to that Bible study and it started a slow and steady chain reaction in my life. Looking back, it blew my mind. There were people my age who genuinely loved Jesus?! And they didn't need what I thought I needed to have a good time?! They actually believed the stuff I grew up learning about. And their parents weren't even making them go! I didn't have a category for that. I didn't realize it at first, but God was beginning to pull me back to Him. He was knocking on my door. I just didn't know it. As soon as I took one step toward God, I began to experience an unexplainable amount of resistance and opposition. From within and without. It's like I unknowingly kicked a hornets nest. Before I was even convinced of the reality of God, I became acutely aware of the reality of some dark, evil forces that were trying to keep me from that Bible study and keep me from getting to know those Christians or moving in that direction.

Addiction urges intensified. Anger and frustration increased. Doubt and depression started rolling in. Party offers and pressure increased. It was both odd and obvious. Some strange "phenomena" took place. It was, for me, an undeniable, unmistakable all out war. Something or someone "real" was working against me and didn't want me to move toward God.

I wasn't even totally sure about God and Jesus at this point... but Satan convinced me he was real first! "If spiritual forces and darkness were real," I thought, "and if Satan is real, and the spiritual realm is real...that must mean there is something or Someone real and good on the other side that he is trying to keep me from."

"If Satan is real, then God is real too," I thought.

Maybe you've heard the phrase, "The greatest trick the devil ever pulled was convincing the world he didn't exist."

By God's grace, I realized the devil existed and even worse, I was actually currently on his team. And he wasn't about to just let me walk away. Like Pharaoh with the Israelites. He clinched down harder.

He's a loser, but he hates losing. He got ticked. And it showed. And that simultaneously scared me and convinced me that I needed to get right with God. I needed Jesus to help me, forgive me, and save me. I needed to get on the right side of this battle. I needed to get on the winning team—God's Team.

So I started running toward Jesus. Crying out for Him to save me. I found an old Bible and pulled it out in my room alone late at night. I didn't know where to start, but I remember someone had told me when I was growing up in church that if you opened to the very middle you'd be in the book of Psalms. So I thought I'd give that a try. I started reading and it was like someone was reading my thoughts. I could hardly put it down. It was eerie how the prayers and cries for help, the pleas for salvation and deliverance from a powerful enemy by this David guy were exactly what I was thinking and experiencing.

Finally, I got to Psalm 18 and read about God thundering from Heaven to route the enemy and rescue the one crying out. On April 22, 1997, I knew that Jesus had heard my prayer and rescued me and delivered me to the winning side of this cosmic battle. I call it my white flag day of surrender. My life has never been the same. That fall, I met the girl who would become my wife. And I met my closest friend and brother in Christ. And I met my lifelong mentor and friend. 11 years later we planted a church together and we're 14+ years into that incredible journey of seeing Jesus change lives and save and transform hundreds of men who are being set free by Jesus and becoming and building Stronger Men.

Satan's blatant attempts to resist and oppose me lead to the Holy Spirit convincing me, the Father hearing me, and Jesus saving me. I'll stop short of thanking Satan, but I'm grateful God directed the devil's bullet into his own foot, yet again.

Adam, 45

REFLECT & DISCUSS

1. How have you been made aware of spiritual reality and spiritual war in your life?

2. What stands out to you most about Satan from the passage in Revelation 12?

3. Are there any current strategies or tactics you feel the enemy is using to try to accuse, deceive, or discourage you? Where is the enemy currently bringing resistance into your life?

4. What would it look like for you to walk in greater victory?

WEEK TWO

5. How or why is it helpful to understand these truths about Satan?

_____
_____
_____

6. What do men in particular need to know or remember from this passage? This chapter?

_____
_____
_____

7. How does knowing the truth about the nature and tactics of the enemy help us become Stronger Men?

_____
_____
_____

TAKE ACTION

- Write out on a notecard and memorize Revelation 12:11 and Colossians 2:13-15.
- Write out a prayer for your wife and family using truths found in Revelation 12.
- Write out a one-paragraph version of your testimony or spiritual journey as you understand it right now. Share it with a man you look up to in the faith this week.

WEEK 3

EQUIPPED FOR BATTLE

Finally, be strong in the Lord and in His mighty power. Put on the full armor of God, so that you can take your stand against the devil's schemes. For our struggle is not against flesh and blood, but against the rulers, against the authorities, against the powers of this dark world and against the spiritual forces of evil in the heavenly realms.

Therefore put on the full ARMOR OF GOD,

so that when the day of evil comes, you may be able to stand your ground, and after you have done everything, to stand. Stand firm then, with the belt of truth buckled around your waist, with the breastplate of righteousness in place, and with your feet fitted with the readiness that comes from the gospel of peace. In addition to all this, take up the shield of faith, with which you can extinguish all the flaming arrows of the evil one. Take the helmet of salvation and the sword of the Spirit, which is the Word of God. And pray in the Spirit on all occasions with all kinds of prayers and requests. With this in mind, be alert and always keep on praying for all the Lord's people. Pray also for me, that whenever I speak, words may be given me so that I will fearlessly make known the mystery of the gospel, for which I am an ambassador in chains. Pray that I may declare it fearlessly, as I should.

EPHESIANS 6:10-20

Let me point out the obvious: Stronger Men aren't actually strong. They're weak.

Yes, you're weak. And if you know that, you have a prayer at making it out alive.

There's only one source of strength for spiritual war. "Be strong in THE LORD and in HIS mighty power."

Whose strength is it? Whose power is it?

The Lord's. Period. Don't forget it.

The minute we as men puff out our chest in a display of macho-man egotistical strength should be the moment we all wince and cringe. Because we all know what comes next.

You'd think we'd learn by now? But there's a reason the internet continues to be daily replenished with shorts and reels and stories and memes of dudes faceplanting, crashing, flopping, falling, and failing.

P-R-I-D-E.

The call to Stronger Manhood, and to victorious living in the spiritual battle we face, is a call to humble yourself, admit your weakness, and find your strength DAILY in THE LORD.

Not only does He offer us His strength and power, but He equips us with the armor we need if we are going to stand against the devil's schemes.

Your enemy was up before you. Scheming. He's already laid down traps for you today. When you wake up each morning, the fiery arrows are already in the air...heading your way. There are arrows heading toward your head, your heart, your wife, your family, your pastor, your church. Stronger Men KNOW that. And they know the arrows are real, hot, sharp, and that it sucks to get shot.

So, fellas, let's suit up. Every day.

In humility, take up the armor.

With conviction, STAND UP today. There's a fight coming in the spirit.

The battle is not against flesh and blood...this is a spiritual battle with forces of evil in an unseen realm.

Your head needs to get right. Your heart needs to be all in. Your name is being called—you're being called to the front line.

WEEK THREE

My heart rate just increased a bit. And that's how a Stronger Man feels at some point every day.

Like the moment you're about to jump out of a plane. The moment you take the football field for kick off. The moment the gun goes off and the race starts. Or the moment you head out the door to start your patrol shift. Or the ambulance shows up and is bringing in your next ER patient. Or your wife just called and her water broke. Or it's time to talk to your son about sex.

You get the point. It's "go time."

For Stronger Men, it's that way every day our feet hit the floor.

Before we go any further, let's do a brief "check" of the equipment we're given. Picture a Roman soldier in all his gear. That's what Paul had in mind.

BELT OF TRUTH

The belt holds everything in place. Without the truth, it all falls down. Stronger Men are soldiers committed to truth—The Truth. The enemy only traffics in lies. He's the father of lies. Stronger Men traffic in truth. It's loving to be a protector who doesn't leave the truth behind. Without the truth, it's a losing battle. Be ready to stand for the truth today.

BREASTPLATE OF RIGHTEOUSNESS

Protect your heart. Protect your integrity. Protect your conscience. The enemy always aims some of his arrows at the heart of men. He wants you to believe you're a guilty failure. Or get you to act like one. He wants you to feel like a loser. Or get you to act like one. But Jesus has given His men His righteousness. The old is gone the new has come. Walk in the protection and power of righteousness. Don't let the enemies arrows and condemning whispers pierce your confidence in Christ. Be ready to believe and do the right thing today.

BOOTS OF GOSPEL READINESS

Are you ready and able to talk about Jesus? Make sure your feet are fitted with the readiness to bring the gospel message of peace. We may be willing to go to war, but we can't forget we are actually fighting to bring the peace of Christ to more souls today. How beautiful are the feet of those who bring good news! The message of the gospel brings peace with God and can make enemies brothers. Be ready to be an ambassador of reconciliation and peace today. The best soldiers are men who love peace and can talk about the peace Jesus has brought to their own soul, even while being capable of war with the enemy to protect those in harms way. Be ready to talk about the good news of Jesus today.

SOLDIER

SHIELD OF FAITH

The shield of faith is what extinguishes the fiery arrows. Faith in the promises of God, in the faithfulness of God, protects. It's our greatest defense against the attacks. By faith, the ancients of Hebrews 11 conquered and were commended. By faith we resist the enemy, say no to sin, walk in obedience and live to fight another day. Be ready to raise the shield of faith today.

HELMET OF SALVATION

The enemy also always aims for the head. Stop and think. Make your calling and election sure. Know that you know that you know that your helmet of salvation is on and you're not taking it off. In Christ, you ARE a helmet-wearing, blood-bought soldier. Guard your thoughts. Keep your wits about you. Be ready to think and act like a saved man today.

SWORD OF THE SPIRIT

This is the one piece of offensive equipment. The sword. The Word of God. Don't leave home without it. In your mind and in your heart, so you can wield it in your hand against the dragon. Jesus combatted temptation in the wilderness with the Word of God..."*it is written!*" (see **Matthew 4:1-11**). Know the Word and, with it, be increasingly ready to slay the dragon today. You will need to swing the Sword today. Get a good grip.

As an equipped soldier, fitted for battle, here are Paul's two final exhortations:

1. Be alert and always keep on praying. Pray throughout your day today.

"Father, show me where You're at work around me today."

"Father, help me to honor You today."

"Jesus, be with my wife today. My son. My daughter."

"Lord, give me Your strength today...fill me with Your power."

"Holy Spirit, keep me sharp and alert today."

"Father, let Your peace rule in my heart. Guide my actions and words today."

"Lord, lead me through the chaos today. Protect me."

"Lord, thank You for being with me. Be with _____ today in a special way."

2. Fearlessly make known the mystery of the gospel.

"Would you like to come to church with me this week?"

"A group of my friends and I get together every week to talk about what God is doing in our lives, would you like to join us sometime?"

"Each month, all the men at my church come together to spur each other on to be Stronger Men, better husbands, fathers, leaders and men, you should come."

"I'd love to tell you more about how I got through that time in my life, how I've experienced big changes in my life with that issue, and what Jesus has done in my life and my family."

LET'S PRAY

Lord, strengthen me to fight the good fight today. Help me rely on You and use the armor You've given us to stand firm today. Fill me with Your Holy Spirit. Equip my head, heart, and hands for the battles I face. Help me stay alert. In Jesus' Name, amen.

SOLDIER

FROM A STRONGER MAN

I spent 17 years of my life being addicted to drugs and alcohol. Addiction nearly destroyed my life and my marriage. I almost lost everything. Satan wanted to destroy me. Sin had a grip on me.

My wife kicked me out of the house and I defiantly went to rehab. I was soft and I wanted to quit. I was mentally, physically, and spiritually weak. After a month of hiding my fear with anger and pride, I was introduced to the Word. I met Jesus for the first time. I learned what it really means to have a personal relationship with God. It didn't take long for God to light a fire in my mind and heart and show me it was time to fight. I gave my life to Jesus and realized that He had truly won the battle—I only had to surrender to Him and trust Him and follow Him and get on the right side of the war. With God providing the strength, I fought. I fought for my life. I fought for my marriage. I fought for my three kids. I finally got to go back home!

Today, it's not perfect but my wife loves and respects me. My kids have a father. I've been sober for over 7 years. The enemy is around every corner, and I can't let my guard down. I know I need to keep fighting the battle every day. **I surround myself with godly people. I seek strength from God's Word. I walk in the light and run like hell from the temptations of the enemy.** I get to tuck my kids in bed every night. I'm living proof that Jesus can set you free and that you don't have to let the enemy keep you bound and defeated. Life's not easy, but it is so good! One of my favorite verses is **Joshua 1:9**:

> "Be strong and courageous; do not be frightened and do not be dismayed, for the Lord your God is with you wherever you go."

I'm fighting to be a Stronger Man and punch fear right in the mouth. I am committed to raising my sons (and my daughter) to be who God is calling them to be. But I know I can't do it alone. I know I have to get better. I know I have to continue to work. I know I have to surround myself with Stronger Men who draw their strength from King Jesus!

Jake, 44

"The true soldier fights not because he hates what is in front of him, but because he loves what is behind him."

— GK Chesterton

SOLDIER

REFLECT & DISCUSS

1. What are ways you prepare your mind and heart for the reality of spiritual war every day?

___

2. Where are you experiencing the greatest "attack" currently?

___

3. How have you seen pride set you up a fall in your life? What would a recent example be?

___

4. Describe a time you felt spiritually weak. Describe a time you felt spiritually strong. What did those times teach you?

___

WEEK THREE

5. How can you help equip other men for spiritual battle and victory?

___

6. Which piece of the armor stands out to you today?

___

7. How would you describe your experience with prayer? How can you grow in the area of prayer?

___

TAKE ACTION

- Read Ephesians 6:10-20 each day for the next week and spend at least 5 minutes using it to inform and guide your prayer for yourself and others each day. What did you notice at the end of the week?

- Evaluate your daily routine, especially morning and evening. What's one change you could make this week?

WEEK 4

TAKE EVERY THOUGHT CAPTIVE

For though we live in the world, we do not wage war as the world does. The weapons we fight with are not the weapons of the world. On the contrary, they have **DIVINE POWER** to demolish strongholds. We demolish arguments and every pretension that sets itself up against the knowledge of God, and we take captive every thought to make it **obedient to Christ.**

2 CORINTHIANS 10:3-5

The mind is a battlefield.

Wrong thoughts can really, really do damage. Lives, families, children, even entire nations can be destroyed and held in bondage because of wrong thinking. I think we are seeing that unfold all around us right now.

The Bible is clear. There are two possible motives for our thoughts: rebellion to God or obedience to God.

Rebellious thoughts always lead to strongholds that choke the life out of people. Obedient thoughts lead to freedom that fills your sail and lungs with fresh air.

I have a good friend named Chris. Before I met him, he spent years in and out of prison through his 20s and 30s. On and off drugs. Job to job. Girlfriend to girlfriend. Trouble to trouble.

On one of his stints in prison, he was given a Bible. He had a godly man speak wisdom and truth into his life. He began to read that Bible and listen to wise counsel. His thinking began to change and his life soon followed. **Romans 12** tells us we can "*be transformed by the renewing of your mind*," and that's exactly what happened to my friend Chris. His life has been dramatically transformed!

He's been sober for 7 years. He's grown leaps and bounds in his relationship with Jesus. He's been baptized, mentored, discipled, and has literally changed his thinking in every area of his life. He decided to approach relationships according to the Bible's guidance and godly counsel, and he's now married to a godly woman. It's truly an incredible and inspiring story.

A police officer, like the ones he used to fight, hate, and get arrested by, was his best man in his wedding. Chris and his wife just welcomed their first child, well, first two children—they now have twin boys!

You might be surprised, though, to hear that he still goes to jail a lot. Not as an inmate but as the chaplain for our county's regional jail. He sits across the glass from inmates who sit where he used to sit. He then pulls the keys from his pocket, and filled with grace and truth, he says, "I used to be where you are, but now, they gave me the keys to this place. Are you ready to change your life? You can. God can. You only have to change one thing. Everything."

And he proceeds to tell them about Jesus and ask them if they want to pursue a relationship with God.

Chris is no longer a captive. Instead, he started taking his thoughts captive.

You and I need to do the same thing every day.

WEEK FOUR

You may not be in the shape Chris was, but that doesn't mean you don't have strongholds in your life.

You and I are one bad thought away, one bad choice away from a ton of pain. I see it all the time. On the faces of wives and children who bear the burden of weak men in their lives.

We see it in the Church: the decline of biblical backbone and the rise of cowardly compromise in the face of an activist culture.

We see it in our communities, where ungodly policies, from darkened hearts and rebellious minds, put society on the road to increasing filth and ruin.

It's not ultimately a political problem, though politics certainly play a part. It's a rebellion problem. A spiritual sin problem. A thinking problem.

Men need mental armed guards and checkpoints. Day and night. We need to once again become the gate keepers of our families, churches, and communities.

The primary battle going on in the world is not a physical war, it's a spiritual one. There are times when men need to physically defend themselves and others, but the Christian man doesn't seek that fight out. He primarily fights a different kind of battle. With different weapons.

A.W. Tozer said the most important thing about someone is what comes into their mind when they think about God.

Men need to guard the gate of their thoughts the way a customs agent checks out those entering the country. Or an airport its potential passengers. Or a bouncer at an exclusive uptown party.

You don't just let anyone and everyone walk right in.

Men, you need to interrogate your thoughts. *Where did you come from? Why are you here? What is the nature of your business here? Do you have any bitterness or jealousy? Any fruitcake ideas or lust that dulls the senses? Can I see some ID? I'm going to need to search your bag.*

And when you find one that is suspicious or is found to have dangerous and nefarious intent and would lead you into sin...you take it captive, gain its submission, violently if need be, and you turn it on its head.

The enemy wants you to lust after that woman in the store. Did you know it's possible to pray for her instead as you look away? Then turn your thoughts and begin praying for your wife and thanking God for the gift of your wife and ask Him to help you be a godly man who is filled with purity and integrity and a blessing to his family.

Men need to feel the weight of being an example for the entire Church. *If every man at my church had my thought life, how strong would our church be?*

Can you imagine if every man thought that way? How strong would the men become? How strong would the marriages become? How happy and safe and protected and cherished would the wives be? How strong would the Church become?

When the voice in your head starts to argue with and disrespect your wife in a defensive tone, you step in. When pride puffs up and you start thinking of all you deserve and how mistreated you are, arrest those thoughts.

"Stop right there! You want to bring conflict into my marriage and chaos into my house. You want to fuel pride in my mind and self-righteousness in my heart. I don't follow you any more, you self-

defending, self-serving, others-belittling, marriage-killing, God-defying thoughts. **Get behind me, Satan**. *I can smell the fire of hell on your clothes. I don't let your kind in here anymore. Instead, I choose to listen carefully. To hear what my wife is saying and understand what she needs. I recognize the truth she is pointing out and my part in the problem. I'm going to choose to respond in humility and thank her for sharing her thoughts and feelings with me. If there's anything I'm unclear on, I'm going to humbly seek understanding and clarity. If there's anything I truly disagree on or we need to work through, I'm going to speak with gentleness and make clear that my goal is unity in the truth and oneness in the Spirit. I'm ready to admit when and where I'm wrong. I'll apologize, own my sinful behavior, attitude, or speech, ask for forgiveness, and affirm her role as helper in my life. I'm willing to allow other voices of godly counsel to weigh in if we can't resolve it."*

Do you think that kind of thinking would make a difference? Do you think these are small matters? They're huge.

I have a fundamental conviction, based on God's design in Scripture, that when the men get stronger everything gets better.

There's plenty of sociological research that bears that out. The greatest social ills in society have a direct link to the demise of strong, noble, and tough-and-tender masculinity. It's true in families, churches, workplaces, and cities.

God is always seeking to raise an army of men. And their mission is to demolish strongholds. What are those strongholds? Arguments, ideas, and lofty opinions that are opposed to the knowledge and truth of God.

In order to get stronger in this area, men need to think. Men need to read. Men need to understand ideas and their consequences. Men need to be able to employ logic and reason and expose an idea whose trajectory is toward error and whose origin is foolish. Men need to humble themselves and seek a renewed and transformed mind.

The gospel is a mighty weapon—it generates a worldview of truth and reality that challenges anyone and any thought that opposes God.

Does this come from the flesh or the Spirit?

Is this in line with the principles of God or the opinions of man?

Does this lead to the character of Christ or the character of self?

WEEK FOUR

Does it puff up or build up?

Does it lead me toward holiness or compromise?

Is this the fruit of the Spirit or the forbidden fruit in the garden?

The writer to the Hebrews exhorts us to pursue obedience to Jesus and to elevate our thinking and become mature through training our minds with the Word of God.

"We have much to say about this, but it is hard to make it clear to you because you no longer try to understand. In fact, though by this time you ought to be teachers, you need someone to teach you the elementary truths of God's Word all over again. You need milk, not solid food! Anyone who lives on milk, being still an infant, is not acquainted with the teaching about righteousness. But solid food is for the mature, who by constant use have trained themselves to distinguish good from evil." **Hebrews 5:11-14**

Let's take every thought captive and be mature in our thinking. That's how we wage war as good soldiers. That's the way of Stronger Men.

LET'S PRAY

Lord, wake me up to the reality of the battlefield of my thoughts. Help me stand guard over my mind and my thoughts and take them captive today. Remind me of what is true and good and right. Help me recognize the lies and arguments of the enemy and my own flesh. Help me grow as a Stronger Man in my thinking. In Jesus' Name, amen.

SOLDIER

FROM A STRONGER MAN

All I cared about growing up was fitting in. I wanted everyone to like me. I wanted everyone to think I was cool. Being accepted was the only thing I cared about—I would do anything to be liked.

When I was 15 years old, I found out that I was adopted and that my "dad" wasn't my "real dad." Boy did that rock my world! I felt like I had been lied to my entire life. I moved out that summer and started hanging out with the 'cool' kids.

Getting high was the cool thing now and so off I went down my road of addiction and crime. I was also trying to fill that part of my identity missing from not having a dad. Drug dealers and gangsters were who I looked up to and who I wanted to be like.

I went to prison three times, rehab five times, and I-don't-know-how-many times to county jails—a lot.

Roughly 8 years of my life was spent in some type of custody against my will, but even when I was out, I was still in a prison of sin. I just didn't know it.

On December 3rd of 2015 in the King County Regional Justice Center, I met Jesus. I gave my life to Him. I was told that when I read my Bible, that's when God speaks to me. And when I pray that's when I speak to Him. So I've been doing that ever since. I moved back home to Wenatchee, found an amazing body of believers at Grace City and have become a new creation.

This past year, I got engaged and married, my wife became pregnant with twin boys, we moved into a new home, our healthy twin boys were born, and I was hired as a pastor at Grace City Church.

My life has been a wild ride since that day back in December of 2015. Although a little confusing to navigate at first, my life with Christ is the surest thing in my life, and all I want to do is give glory to God and help more people meet, love, and follow Jesus!

Chris, 46

WEEK FOUR

> "We want them to know, Heavenly Father, that we die for freedom!"
>
> — *Glory*

REFLECT & DISCUSS

1. What is one thing you've changed your mind about as you've grown in your faith?

2. What are some of the current ideas and arguments in our society that need defeated in the minds of Christians?

3. What are the most common sources of these false ideas and arguments?

4. What is the fruit or evidence of someone who is taken captive by lies and arguments that become strongholds?

WEEK FOUR

5. How can a husband support his wife in this battle?
_____
_____
_____

6. How can a dad protect and support his children in the war for the mind?
_____
_____
_____

7. What are some practical steps you need to take take to protect and purify your thinking?
_____
_____
_____

TAKE ACTION

- Try and keep track each day this week of the times you intentionally reign in and redirect your thoughts.

- Eliminate any source that is contributing to polluted thoughts and ideas about God.

- Write down and memorize 2 Corinthians 10:3-5.

WEEK 5

ACT LIKE MEN

"Be watchful, stand firm in the faith, **ACT LIKE MEN,** be strong. Let all that you do be done in love.

1 CORINTHIANS 16:13-14

Talk about two great verses for men. 1 Corinthians 16:13-14 packs a punch.

Men like to get to the point. So here the Apostle Paul does just that. Five clear exhortations. With the central exhortation holding the two on either side together. *Act like men.*

It holds elements of toughness and tenderness together. It points to the role of men as protectors and lovers. Lions and lambs.

What I love about this verse, and the phrase "act like men," in particular, is that it makes a profound point about manhood.

To be a man is a good thing. Full stop. There's something innately good and noble about "acting like a man."

There's no qualification given. No adjectives applied. It doesn't say, "Act like godly men." Or faithful men. Or noble men. Or good men. It just says, "act like men."

God made men and women on purpose. It's a good design. And before sin entered the picture, being a man came with nobility and a clear job description.

Adam was given the instructions in the garden before Eve was created. It was his job and responsibility to initiate and lead her spiritually and morally. And to protect and provide for her physically and emotionally.

But when the serpent enters the story, he goes around Adam and starts chatting with Adam's wife. And Adam does nothing. In that moment, he was failing as a man. He wasn't protecting. He wasn't providing. He wasn't leading. He wasn't loving.

He was passive.

Eve has her own responsibility too, to be sure. And Satan gets dealt with as well. God hands out consequences to all. There's plenty to go around. But there's no avoiding Adam failed to do his job. And then tried to pass the buck.

Men are not that sophisticated. The garden is repeated again and again by passive men who fail to act like men.

The call to "be a man" must be given carefully and clearly.

It encompasses a very important role.

How are you doing at being a man?

WEEK FIVE

As you read this, in this moment and season of your life, where do you need to step up? Where do you need to get stronger?

Men need constant encouragement and regular reminders to "act like men."

We should never hear that and think, "yeah, yeah, I know, I know." That would be a warning sign.

We can drift so fast. Our battle is a DAILY one.

Every time I'm exhorted or encouraged or someone checks in with me to see "how I'm doing"...it's a blessing. Every time.

It's a powerful and important ministry to look another man in the eye, with sincere love and ask, "How are you doing?"

I get the opportunity to speak to men on a regular basis and I'm often moved to simply ask, "Where are you at? How are you doing? Where are you going?" And along with that is, "How can I pray for you? How can I help?"

These are powerful and helpful questions for men.

QUESTION 1: Where are you?

It's the question God came asking when Adam was hiding in his guilt and shame. "Adam, where are you?" It's a question that is used to invite and initiate reflection that can actually lead to salvation and rescue. Where are you at in your relationship with God right now? In your leadership and responsibility as a man? Where are you in the process of growing and getting stronger and moving forward? Where are you in your thinking? Where are you in your degree of focus? Are you running? Hiding? Strong? Struggling? Where are you in your role and journey as a man? With your family? Are you being watchful? Are you standing firm?

QUESTION 2: How are you doing?

Out of the overflow of the heart the mouth speaks. When a man is asked how he is doing by another man—not in a casual drive-by kind of way, but in an honest, "checking in" kind of way—he has a choice to make. Be honest or blow smoke. It can be a powerful gift. Don't get me wrong, not every exchange with men needs to press to go deep. I don't believe that. In fact, I can even find it annoying and tiresome. You can tell if someone is "trying too hard." Time, place, relationship, and trust matter. But we all need men in our life who are regularly asking us this question. Men are stronger when they are self-aware and honest.

SOLDIER

Question 3: Where are you going?

As in, in the last week, month, or range of time since we've talked, how's your trajectory and trend? Are you still heading North (in line with God's will and call on your life)? Or have you started to drift? Are there any temptations that you're entertaining that are starting to pull you into danger? Are there any distractions or commitments that are starting to mess with your priorities? Is there any area of your life where you're starting to wander off the right path?

Pay attention to these things, men. Or as Paul says, **be watchful**.

Stand firm in the faith. Don't waver. Don't drift. Hold tight to Jesus.

Be strong. Stay courageous. Endure hardship. Carry the weight you're called to carry.

Let all that you do be done in love. Be a man who is both strong

WEEK FIVE

and safe. Tough and tender. Capable of holy violence and capable of gentleness and compassion.

In other words: **ACT LIKE MEN.**

LET'S PRAY

Lord, thank You for making me a man. Help me act like a man. Give me eyes to see where I need to grow stronger. Help me be watchful of the temptations and distractions that come. Give me strength to bear the weight of a man who is following Jesus. Help me stand firm in the faith. Make me a tough and tender protector. In Jesus' Name, amen.

SOLDIER

FROM A STRONGER MAN

As I get older and I look back on my life and my years as a teenager and young adult, one of my favorite scriptures is **Psalms 25:7**—"*remember not the sins of my youth and my transgressions.*" I pray that often. And as I think about that in relationship to being a Stronger Man and the call to be a soldier, in particular, all I can say is that, in a godly sense, I was no man at all. As for being a soldier, you could easily say I was aiding and abetting the enemy. I knew in my heart what I should be doing but chose to follow a different path. But thanks be to God He was merciful to me—pursued me—and the Holy Spirit continued to work in my heart. Ultimately, Jesus saved me.

One of the things I lacked in my youth was the presence of other godly men in my life. When that changed, pretty much everything changed. I started hanging out with godly men—who, like soldiers, were on mission for something greater than self. Men who knew what and WHO they were fighting for, and men who regularly prepared and armed themselves for battle in God's Word. It was a huge encouragement to me to not be in the fight by myself, but to shoulder up with other men who were on mission. This has spurred me on to dig in and fight the good fight, to be a Stronger Man, not only for the battles that each of us face every day, but also for the mission for others to meet, love, and follow Jesus. **My favorite motto among military rescue groups is, "so others may live."** I love that saying because it reminds me of the ultimate rescue mission that happened some 2000 years ago, when Jesus sacrificed everything so others may live! And now we are free to gear up and be on mission, to carry the fight to the enemy knowing the war is won.

There are times, as a soldier for God, when things can look overwhelming. The outlook for success seems impossible. But I go back to a question I asked years ago and the answer I got from a young pastor named Josh. The question stemmed from two things Jesus said in the Bible: "go and sin no more" and "be holy as your Father in Heaven is holy." Both seemingly impossible. And he answered with a soldier analogy. The short version is this—a special ops group was called in for a mission that consisted of sneaking into enemy territory during the cover of night to capture an enemy general who was held up in the most fortified bunker known to man, surrounded by hundreds of armed guards with layer-upon-layer of impenetrable security. Without going into more detail (there was a lot), the crux of the story was that as the men listened to the assignment there were two things that each of them thought: certain death and impossible suicide mission. They knew they were going to die. Then the commander said something that changed everything, "by the way, I have successfully done this myself, and I'm going with you."

Shawn, 62

SOLDIER

REFLECT & DISCUSS

1. Which one of Paul's phrases in 1 Corinthians 16:13-14 most stands out to you today?

_____
_____
_____

2. Which one do you need to focus on this week?

_____
_____
_____

3. Who are the men in your life who ask you the three questions? Who do you ask? Where could you find those men?

_____
_____
_____

4. How can you become a better watchman?

_____
_____
_____

WEEK FIVE

5. How can you become a tougher man?

6. How can you become a more tender man?

7. Why is it important to be both tough and tender?

TAKE ACTION

- Make note this week of the situations you're in that require you to be more Lion-like (tough) and the situations that require you to be more Lamb-like (tender). Reflect back on those situations. What did you learn?

- Memorize 1 Corinthians 16:13-14.

- Pick 3 men to check in with this week. Ask them one or more of the questions. Listen carefully and offer a word of encouragement and offer to say a short prayer for them. What was the result?

WEEK 6

HUMBLE, ALERT, SOBER

All of you, clothe yourselves with

HUMILITY

toward one another, because, "God opposes the proud but gives grace to the humble."

Humble yourselves, therefore, under God's mighty hand, that He may lift you up in due time. Cast all your anxiety on Him because He cares for you. Be alert and of sober mind. Your enemy the devil prowls around like a roaring lion looking for someone to devour. Resist him, standing firm in the faith, because you know that the family of believers throughout the world is undergoing the same kind of sufferings. And the God of all grace, who called you to His eternal glory in Christ, after you have suffered a little while, will Himself restore you and make you strong, firm and steadfast. To Him be the power forever and ever. Amen.

1 PETER 5:5-11

In 1 Peter 5, we find several vital attributes of Stronger Men.

The Apostle Peter, at the end of his first letter, was writing specifically to men. Old men and young men. He addressed both the elders of God's people and the young men coming up under them.

And he was writing to those who were facing persecution and being scattered and attacked for their faith. "*Strangers in the world.*"

Peter was writing to men in troubled and tumultuous times. We should pay attention.

The starting point is HUMILITY.

Stronger Men clothe themselves in humility because they know that God opposes the proud, but gives grace to the humble.

Pride may appear strong on the outside, but its a recipe for failure. You will only be fighting God. And that never goes well.

WEEK SIX

Men need to grapple with the reality that there are, in fact, many things beyond your control or your ability to change. This can be hard for men to admit. In our pride, we often think we "have the answers." We think, "I got this."

If we let out a warrior's cry in pride and charge in to change the world, we are fools and we will fail.

Men need to embrace their limitations and bow before the true Sovereign King.

God alone is the one with the mighty hand. And if He's not in it, it won't succeed. So humble yourself. You're not going to be the MVP here. That award has already been given. That seat is already taken. And it's not yours. It's God's.

God is the one who has the power to "*lift you up in due time.*"

Humble yourselves before the Lord and toward one another. You're not "The Man." Jesus is The Man. Your strength and victory are only possible in, with, and under the Hand of God.

Have you ever knelt before the Lord? "*God, here I am. I am nothing without You. Forgive me for my arrogant and foolish pride. Root out the pride in my life and make me a humble man of God. I do not want to oppose You. I need Your grace. I surrender to You. I submit to You. I will trust in Your perfect plan and in Your power to lead me and lift me up in Your time. I'm frustrated and anxious about the way things are and the things beyond my control. Today, I choose to cast all of my anxiety on You. Thank You that You care for me and for what is good and right even more than I do. Lead me today...*"

That's a Stronger Man's prayer. And from that place of humility, you're ready to face the day, take your stand, and resist the enemy. Now you're in the right posture to stand and fight.

But the Christian life is not a "one and done" prayer. You don't "set it and forget it" and walk away mindlessly.

You must stay alert and go about your day with a sober mind.

The devil is prowling around like a roaring lion looking for someone to devour. Your mind needs to be sharp. You have to stay on your toes, keep your head on a swivel and keep your wits about you.

Men notoriously struggle with sobriety. And there are many things that can intoxicate the mind of a man. Too much alcohol or foreign substances that alter the mind are a no-brainer. And if that's your vulnerability, you need to deal with it. But there are other things that intoxicate a man. Money, sex, power, ego, attention, image, and success can also cloud a man's soul. Whatever your drug/idol of choice...the call to men is to resist. Stay sober. Stay humble. Be alert.

Without a sober mind you won't see the enemy slip into your camp. You won't be sharp. You'll leave the gate open. And you'll let the enemy in.

And it's your responsibility as a man to keep watch. To close the gate. To protect your mind, your heart, your family, your home. What comes into your house, what entertains your children, is on your watch.

It's much easier to stand your ground when you know you aren't standing alone. You're in a well-worn battlefield. Your brothers and sisters around the world are facing similar attacks or worse. Hold the line! Stand your ground! Endure suffering! Don't give in.

God Himself will carry you through the finish. In the end, He will restore you and make you strong, firm, and steadfast. Your hope to make it is found in His grace, His promise, and His power.

LET'S PRAY

Lord, help me choose to clothe myself in humility today. I need Your grace, strength, help, power, and love in my life. Without You, I'll make a mess of it all. Give me a sober and alert mind, to be vigilant throughout the day, watching for the enemy's attack. Help me resist him and stand firm. In Jesus' Name, amen.

"There are two equal and opposite errors into which our race can fall about the devils. One is to disbelieve in their existence. The other is to believe, and to feel an excessive and unhealthy interest in them."

— C.S. Lewis

SOLDIER

"For God and Country" is the motto of the US Army Chaplain. My father served our country as a Chaplain for 25 years. He grew up on a farm in Nebraska and learned to love running later in life. So, he's my role model for the "soldier/farmer/athlete/son" profile we talk about in Stronger Man Nation (SMN).

As our country/culture continues to change/decline over the decades since my dad was a soldier, one thing remains true: there is a fierce spiritual battle being waged for the souls of a lost and fallen world. We read about it and see it every day. It's sad but not surprising if you understand what the Bible teaches us about the times we are living in. SMN "soldiers" have to do our part to protect and defend the things that matter most: our marriages, families, and relationships. People and your purpose matter infinitely more than your pride and possessions. For SMN "soldiers" to engage and defeat the enemy, it requires an equally fierce and spiritual response.

A SMN "soldier" shares many characteristics with a military soldier. The soldier ethos I remember from growing up in a military home were guys who were orderly, disciplined, hardworking, determined, persevering, and tough. There was a willingness to make the ultimate sacrifice—giving their life for their country—if necessary. Military soldiers are unique in many ways. SMN "soldiers" are unique in different ways. Fundamentally, we are fighting for sinners to repent, for God's truth to be known, for lost people to be found, for Jesus to be followed. We focus on individual battles. God has promised His followers He will win the war.

But here's the thing, men: if you don't have a "teachable spirit" and are unwilling to submit and learn from excellent, godly, biblically-smart teachers, you are going to fail. You'll fall way short in your role as husband, father (or a single guy) and most importantly, as a follower of Jesus Christ. This is a brief life you have on earth. Unfortunately, that was me in my youth and even into early adulthood. I did not have that "teachable spirit." Didn't always learn what I was being taught. Made way too many selfish decisions. Hurt far too many people. Disobeyed God and sinned. Essentially, I was AWOL (Absent WithOut Leave) from living a SMN life. I had my priorities all wrong. The things the enemy uses to take us away from our faith, all were deployed and all pretty much worked. My marriage was failing. It was time to decide which path I would follow. Thankfully, my wife had not given up on me or our marriage. She had been praying as the Bible commanded her to pray: without ceasing. My dad, as he was battling cancer, intervened and helped me fight for my marriage. As did many other family members. The choice was always obvious—Jesus, wife, and family over everything else. I re-dedicated my life to Jesus, asked for forgiveness, was shown grace-upon-grace, and am eternally grateful and thankful.

Men, true healing and redemption is only available through Jesus Christ! Everything else is the enemy lying and deceiving you. Jesus receives and redeems. Enemy deceives and denies. The choice or path is obvious!

Steve, 63

SOLDIER

REFLECT & DISCUSS

1. What battles are you facing this week?

2. What weighs you down the most right now? What anxieties are rising in your mind and heart?

3. What's the status on your pride vs. humility?

4. What in your life might be clouding your mind/judgment?

5. How has God shown you His grace, His care, or His power in your life? How has He shown you in the last month? Week?

_____
_____
_____

6. How have you experienced God's restoring and strengthening grace in a time of suffering?

_____
_____
_____

7. Who in your life do you need to approach and engage with a more humble attitude? What would that look or sound like? Write it down and look for an opportunity to practice it this week.

_____
_____
_____

TAKE ACTION

- What do you need to limit or eliminate in your life? Identify it and follow through this week.
- In light of this passage, what conversation do you need to initiate with your family (spouse, son, daughter, all together)? Set a time to share what's on your heart and lead that conversation.

WEEK 7

UNDERSTAND AUTHORITY, FAITH, & OBEDIENCE

When Jesus had entered Capernaum, a centurion came to Him, asking for help. "Lord," he said, "my servant lies at home paralyzed, suffering terribly."

Jesus said to him, "Shall I come and heal him?"

The centurion replied, "Lord, I do not deserve to have you come under my roof. But just say the word, and my servant will be healed. For I myself am **a man under authority**, with soldiers under me. I tell this one, 'Go,' and he goes; and that one, 'Come,' and he comes. I say to my servant, 'Do this,' and he does it."

When Jesus heard this, He was amazed and said to those following Him, "Truly I tell you, I have not found anyone in Israel **with such great faith.** I say to you that many will come from the east and the west, and will take their places at the feast with Abraham, Isaac and Jacob in the Kingdom of Heaven. But the subjects of the kingdom will be thrown outside, into the darkness, where there will be weeping and gnashing of teeth."

Then Jesus said to the centurion, "Go! Let it be done just as you believed it would." And his servant was healed at that moment.

MATTHEW 8:5-13

SOLDIER

Jesus had just finished preaching the Sermon on the Mount, the most famous sermon in the world.

He comes down the mountain and immediately the ministry action picks up. Healing after healing after healing.

This Roman centurion soldier certainly stands out. Jesus Himself said, "*I tell you the truth, I have not found anyone in Israel with such great faith.*"

This soldier recognized the power and authority of Jesus. He understood that in order to become a good soldier, you have to follow orders and respect proper spiritual authority.

You have to get authority issues right. How you conduct yourself, whether in or under authority, is a big deal to God.

Hebrews 13:17 says, "*Obey your leaders and submit to their authority. They keep watch over you as men who must give an account. Obey them so that their work will be a joy, not a burden, for that would be of no advantage to you.*"

How do you do with authority? Do you respect or rebel? Do you recognize genuine authority and humbly submit to godly authority in your life? Or do you balk, go rogue, or try and feel more manly by bossing others around?

How do you do in authority? Are you thoughtful or reckless? Arrogant or a servant? Do you recognize that you will give an account of how you lead?

Remember, you're only as good *in* authority as you are *under* authority.

And everyone submits to someone else, eventually.

Good soldiers are not rogue, lone rangers. That may look cool in the movies,

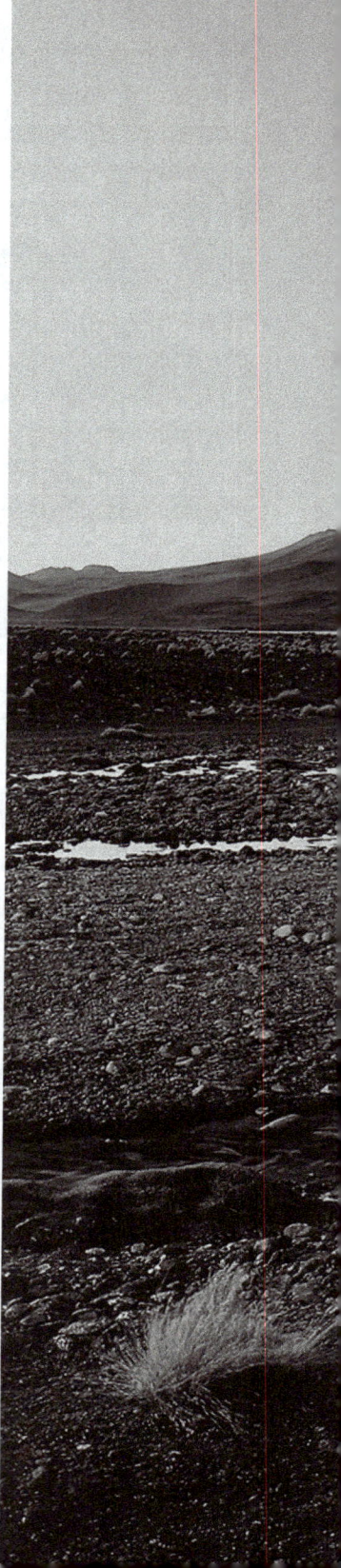

WEEK SEVEN

but in the real world, it's how people die.

And good commanders are not harsh, arbitrary, and demeaning.

Stronger Men know how to follow orders and submit to proper godly authority. And they know how to humbly lead others, caring for their followers, and exercising true strength as exemplary men.

To be a good leader, you have to learn to be a good follower. To be trusted with authority, you have to be trustworthy under authority.

Jesus is a trustworthy Commanding Officer and His Word accomplishes what He intends it to accomplish.

The Roman centurion understood spiritual authority and knew that Jesus only had to say the word and His will would be done. He had faith in the power of Jesus' authority.

How do you become a man who can recognize and respond in a wise and godly way to true spiritual authority?

Once again, it starts with **humility**.

He came asking for help. That takes humility.

He said, "Lord, I do not deserve to have you come under my roof." That's humility.

Secondly, it takes **desire**. Not only did he recognize his need for help and that he was in over his head but he wanted to see his servant helped and healed. He had godly desire to serve and help others.

Third, he had straight-forward, simple **faith**. What made his faith "great" in the eyes of Jesus? It wasn't the size and strength of his faith, but the simplicity, purity, and object of it. "Just say the word and my servant will be healed." His faith was in the person and authority of Jesus and the power of His word. Good soldiers under the centurion did what he said; they followed orders. He believed Jesus had that kind of authority, even over sickness.

And fourthly, he knew that **obedience** is the fruit of genuine faith. Obedience is one of the keys that unlocks the power of God's Word in our lives.

In **John 13**, after washing His disciple's feet, serving the ones under His authority, Jesus Himself said, *"Now that you know these things, you will be blessed if you DO THEM."*

Knowing is one thing. But *doing* is where the blessing comes.

Over and over again, you see these 4 prerequisites for healing in Jesus' ministry.

HUMILITY: Do you know you're in over your head? That you need help?

Often, people reach the point of humility through an overwhelming sense of their need. At that point, they are willing to press through the crowds. They are willing to cry out in desperation. They have nothing to lose and everything to gain. They refuse to carry it on their own, and they run to Jesus.

DESIRE: Do you actually want to grow or change or see others helped and healed?

Jesus regularly asked people, "What do you want me to do for you?" Some people choose to stay unhealthy. They choose their dysfunction. They don't actually want to change. Jesus regularly tests our desire.

FAITH: Do you believe that Jesus has the power and is willing to help?

Some know they are in need, and desire to change and grow, but they're uncertain if Jesus can make any difference. Faith is what moves mountains.

OBEDIENCE: Are you willing to obey whatever Jesus tells you to do? Do you submit to His authority in your life?

Here is where the rubber meets the road. Are you willing to follow through and obey whatever Jesus says? In Jesus' first miracle, turning water into wine (John 2), His mother, Mary, told the servants at the wedding, "Do whatever He tells you." If He tells you to get jugs, get jugs. If He tells you to fill them with water, fill them with water.

It's amazing what Jesus can do with our simple obedience.

Humility, desire, faith, and obedience are what put you in proper relationship with God's authority and put you in the path for Jesus' power to work in and through your life.

This isn't a recipe for "name it and claim it." And it isn't a call to submit to evil or abusive authority. It's about being faithful and available for God to work in your life and use you in the lives of others.

It's the way of a good soldier. The way of a Stronger Man.

LET'S PRAY

Lord, give me humility and faith like the Roman centurion. To trust in the power of Your authority and to submit to Your Word. Help me walk in the blessing of obedience, not the foolishness of rebellion. Help me to be faithful under Your authority, so I can be trusted as a man with authority, and be a godly leader in others' lives. Have Your way in my life today. In Jesus' Name, amen.

SOLDIER

My identity as a soldier means two things to me:

1. I am now enlisted.

Being enlisted means I obey everything my commanding officer tells me to do. I trust in His leadership, and my new life looks very different from my former "civilian" life.

Submission, obedience, and discipline are the new standards I adhere to.

- I am submitted to God's direction and calling on my life and make my mission accomplishing His mission—namely, discipling my own heart, leading my wife and kids into deeper faith, building up the Church, advancing the Kingdom, and sharing the love of Jesus with non-believers.

- I am obedient to His commands written in Holy Scripture. It is no longer up for debate—His principles and truths are supreme, and my duty and delight are to know them and follow them.

- I am disciplined. Growing in spiritual discipline is essential to faithfully fulfilling the station God has given me. It is my responsibility to be prayed up, read up, and filled up with the Holy Spirit in order to be effective and prepared for battle.

2. Jesus is my Warrior King.

Spiritual warfare is real. The battle is fierce. We have a powerful adversary. But in the end, our King is triumphant.

- **Ephesians 6:2** says, "*Our struggle is not against flesh and blood, but against the rulers, against the authorities, against the powers of this dark world and against the spiritual forces of evil in the heavenly realms.*" This directs our minds and hearts to where the war is waged and who it is against.

- **2 Corinthians 10:3-5** says, "*For though we live in the world, we do not wage war as the world does. The weapons we fight with are not the weapons of* *the world. On the contrary, they have divine power to demolish strongholds. We demolish arguments and every pretension that sets itself up against the knowledge of God, and we take captive every thought to make it obedient to Christ."* Again, our war is in the spiritual realm. Our weapons are empowered by the divine power of Christ.

- Before defeating Goliath and the Philistine army in **1 Samuel 17:47**, David (who would later be a king) said, *"All those gathered here will know that it is not by sword or spear that the Lord saves; for the battle is the Lord's."*

Jesus came into this world as a Lamb. He is returning with a sword. He is fighting and winning my battles and will ultimately be victorious over sin, death, evil, and the evil one. All my allegiance belongs to Jesus—my Warrior King.

Sam, 31

REFLECT & DISCUSS

1. What were your first examples of "authority" like in your life?

2. What are some examples from your own journey of good and bad responses to authority or expressions of authority in your life?

3. How would you describe good authority? What makes a good leader?

4. How would you describe bad authority? What makes a bad leader?

WEEK SEVEN

5. What mistakes have you made in relationship to authority?
___
___

6. Of the 4 prerequisites—humility, desire, faith, obedience—which do you need to focus on or grow in most right now?
___
___

7. Where do you need to seek help right now in your life? Who will you talk to about it this week?
___
___
___

TAKE ACTION

- Is there anyone you need to apologize to: any sinful attitude or careless speech you've expressed as one in or under authority recently? If so, follow through this week to humble yourself and apologize, asking for forgiveness.

- Identify a person in your life or sphere of influence this week who needs practical help. Do something about it. Give of your time, energy, skill, ability, or resources to take action to help someone else in a specific way. The Roman centurion was no doubt a busy man with plenty of responsibilities, yet he went out of his way to contact Jesus and seek help for his servant. Who will you do that for this week?

WEEK 8

WHEN STRONGER MEN DON'T GO OUT TO WAR

In the spring, at the time when kings go off to war, David sent Joab out with the king's men and the whole Israelite army. They destroyed the Ammonites and besieged Rabbah. **But David remained in Jerusalem.**

One evening David got up from his bed and walked around on the roof of the palace. From the roof he saw a woman bathing. The woman was very beautiful, and David sent someone to find out about her. The man said, "She is Bathsheba, the daughter of Eliam and the wife of Uriah the Hittite." Then David sent messengers to get her.

2 SAMUEL 11:1-4

SOLDIER

When men choose not to go to war everyone suffers.

At the time when kings go off to war, David remained in Jerusalem.

And that, brothers, was a tragic error.

Learn from David's negative example and do not make the same mistake.

David's sin with Bathsheba (and the compounding nature of sin that followed) stands as a dramatic and important story for men to consider carefully.

Where did David fail?

→ **He failed to go to war. He stopped fighting.**

→ **He sent someone else to do his job.**

→ **He dropped his guard.**

→ **He forfeited his strength.**

→ **He got lazy. He got lax.**

→ **He embraced comfort over conviction.**

→ **He had too much idle time.**

→ **He was up late at night, vulnerable to temptation.**

→ **He let his eyes drift to a woman who wasn't his wife.**

→ **He used his influence and power to take what wasn't his for his own selfish gratification.**

→ **He tried to cover his tracks. He tried to hide his sin.**

WEEK EIGHT

→ **He compounded his sin with more sin.**

→ **He became blind to the brutal reality of what he had done in the eyes of God.**

→ **He opened the door to years of devastation and pain in his family and in the lives of others.**

It's a sobering story. And it's still happening today. In fact, it's all too common.

Brothers, the consequences of not going to battle, of not staying vigilant and not staying on the front lines, are devastating.

The palace of success and comfort can be more dangerous and deadly than the front lines of war, and the bears and lions of David's youthful days as a valiant shepherd.

We have to stay vigilant as warriors. In the fight. Every. Day.

Our past victories do not guarantee today's success or tomorrow's strength. Each day has enough trouble of its own. Every day requires us to show up and fight.

And notice what happened as the story progressed. The sin only grew. It only got worse. David ended up having Bathsheba's noble husband, Uriah, killed. The baby, that was conceived, died. The consequences rippled through David's family.

And it all started by David, the great warrior who slew Goliath, putting down his sword and failing to go to war.

Where are you vulnerable? Where are you following in the slippery steps of David?

There is much to learn and glean from this story.

From the nature of sin to the nature of specific sins to the nature of men's particular vulnerabilities to the mercy of God who pursues David to prophetically expose him in his sin to the nature of genuine repentance to the grace of God who forgives David to the reality of enduring consequences of sin and even to the hope of life after a fall.

There is much to learn. But this is serious business, isn't it?

The prophet Nathan was sent by the Lord (see 2 Samuel 12) to tell David the story of a rich man who had flocks and herds yet killed a

poor man's only ewe lamb to feed a traveling visitor. David, in anger, said, "As surely as the Lord lives the man who did this deserves to die!"

Nathan, seizing on the irony and hypocrisy of David's anger, turned and said to David, "You are the man!"

And the Lord said, "You did it in secret (sinned), but I will do this thing (discipline/consequences) in broad daylight before all Israel."

Then David said to Nathan, "I have sinned against the LORD." Read Psalm 51 for David's prayer of confession.

Nathan replied, "The LORD has taken away your sin. You are not going to die."

Wait. You mean to tell me that "just like that"...that easy, David is off the hook? Well, not exactly. Indeed, someone DID die for David's sin. But in mysterious grace, the Lord allowed another, in the future, to take his place. And while there were serious consequences that rolled out, the good news of scandalous grace is that there is indeed forgiveness and pardon waiting on the other side of sincere repentance and godly sorrow.

And if you stumble over such a display of grace, thinking it's unjust for the Lord to just "forgive" David...you have perhaps yet to grapple with the reality of your own sin and either think you have no need of

WEEK EIGHT

forgiveness yourself or think you can accomplish making up for your own sin by your own good works. Or that the Lord fails to deal justly with sin. But that's not how Christianity works. Sin is paid for in full—no one is "getting away" with anything in the end. The Lord will judge or pardon. The difference is found in repentance and faith in a Savior who shed His blood for sin.

Consider: "*While we were yet sinners, Christ died for us*" (**Romans 5:8**).

There is hope. There is grace and there is justice. Both (grace and justice) are found in the cross of Christ.

Let's consider a few final lessons from the negative example of David's sin with Bathsheba:

- Even when you think you sin in secret, you never truly sin in isolation. Sin always affects others.
- Sin is always and ultimately against the Lord. He is the most offended party.
- Never forget, sin exposure is the work of the light. God is on the move. He's providing a merciful opportunity to repent, be forgiven, and be set free.
- The power of forgiveness does not always erase the reality of ongoing painful consequences in this life.
- God can powerfully restore, redeem, and use those who truly repent before the Lord.
- Learning from the sin and mistakes of others and avoiding the pitfalls of the foolish are wise ways to learn and live.

Don't be a sitting duck for Satan and sin... **GO TO WAR.**

LET'S PRAY

Lord, deliver me from the dangers of comfort, laziness, apathy, and idleness. Forgive me for the times I've failed to go to war and help me fully repent for any and all known sin in my life. Keep me from sin and give me a holy fear that moves me to pick up the sword, lift the shield, and move back to the front lines of the fight. In Jesus' Name, amen.

SOLDIER

FROM A STRONGER MAN

On March 3rd, 2005 I heard a lecture at the Northwest Command College by retired FBI Supervisory Special Agent Richard M. Ayres, author of Leading to Make a Difference that became a seminal moment in my life. Richard's talk was entitled, "A Definition of Integrity."

The word "integrity" is a martial word that comes to us from an ancient Roman army tradition. During the time of the 12 Caesars, the Roman army would conduct morning inspections. As the inspecting Centurion would pass in front of each legionnaire, the soldier would strike his right fist upon his armor breast plate that covered his heart. The armor had to be strongest there in order to protect the heart from sword thrusts and from arrow strikes. As the soldier struck his armor, he would shout "integritas" which in Latin means material wholeness, completeness and entirety.

The inspecting Centurion would listen closely for this affirmation and for the ring that well kept armor would give off. Satisfied that the armor was sound and that the soldier beneath was protected, he would move on to the next man.

At about the same time the Praetorians or imperial bodyguards were ascending into power and influence. Drawn from the best "politically correct" soldiers of the legions, they received the finest equipment and armor. They no longer shouted "integritas" to signify that their armor was sound, they shouted "hail Caesar" to signify that there hearts belonged to the imperial personage-not to their unit, nor to an institution or code of ideals. They armored themselves to serve the cause of a single man.

A century passed and the rift between the legion and the imperial guard and its excesses grew larger. To signify the difference between the two organizations, the legionnaires, upon striking their armor would no longer shout "integritas." Instead, they would shout "integer." Integer means undiminished, complete, perfect. It not only indicated that the armor was sound, it also indicated that the soldiers wearing the armor were sound of character. Each was complete in his integrity and was not associated with the immoral conduct that was rapidly becoming the signature of the imperial bodyguard.

The armor of integrity continued to serve the legion well. For over four centuries they held the line against the marauding Goths and Vandals, but by 383 AD the decline that infected the Republic and the imperial guard had its effects upon the legion.

WEEK EIGHT

A 4th century Roman General wrote, "When because of negligence and laziness, parade ground drills were abandoned, the customary armor began to feel heavy since soldiers rarely, if ever wore it. Therefore, they asked the emperor to set aside the breastplate, mail and then the helmets. So, our soldiers fought the Goths without any protection for the heart and were often beaten by archers."

Although there were many disasters, which led to the loss of great cities, no one tried to restore the armor to the infantry. They took their armor off, and when the armor came off so too came their "integrity." It was only a matter of a few years until the legion rotted from within and was unable to hold the frontiers...the barbarians were at the gate.

As believers in Christ, as Christian Soldiers, we are called in **Ephesians 6:11** to *"Put on the full armor of God, that you may be able to stand against the wiles of the devil."* No one can take our armor from us. Only we can take it off and by doing so give up our integrity. King David's failure began not only when he stayed home from the battle, but when he took off his armor—his integrity.

By God's grace I have seen the power and blessing of integrity in my own life, and I have seen the danger and devastation in men I know who chose to take off their armor of integrity in pursuit of temporary pleasures. Throughout my sixty years of walking with Jesus, my fifty-four years of marriage to my noble wife, and my thirty-five years in the field of law enforcement as a Police Officer, Detective, FBI Special Agent, Supervisory Special Agent, and Chief of Operations for a Sheriffs Office, I have seen these tragic stories play out over and over again. As men endeavoring to be Stronger Men, lets keep our integrity intact, and finish the race strong—in the steps of Jesus, the better King who never took off His armor for us!

Clyde, 76

REFLECT & DISCUSS

1. What stands out to you in this week's reading and review of David and Bathsheba?

2. Where might you be vulnerable currently to sin's attack?

3. How vigilant are you being with your idle time, alone time, and discipline and purity of the eyes and heart?

4. Is there any unconfessed or hidden sin in your life? Why is "confession of sin" difficult for most men?

WEEK EIGHT

5. How have you received and experienced God's mercy and grace?

6. What does it look like in practical terms to stay vigilant and go to war?

7. How have you seen the nature of sin in your own life/story?

TAKE ACTION

- What boundaries and measures do you need to put in place to minimize idle time and avoid sinful temptations? Do it this week.

- If there is any hidden sin in your life, confess it to a trusted pastor/leader, brother in the Lord, and/or your wife to help you come clean before the Lord and others.

- What would a "wartime action plan" look like for your life? Write it down.

WEEK 9

PRAY TO GOD AND POST A GUARD

But when Sanballat, Tobiah, the Arabs, the Ammonites and the people of Ashdod heard that the repairs to Jerusalem's walls had gone ahead and that the gaps were being closed, they were very angry. They all plotted together to come and fight against Jerusalem and stir up trouble against it. **But we prayed to our God and posted a guard** day and night to meet this threat.

Therefore I stationed some of the people behind the lowest points of the wall at the exposed places, posting them by families, with their swords, spears and bows. After I looked things over, I stood up and said to the nobles, the officials and the rest of the people, "Don't be afraid of them. Remember the Lord, who is great and awesome, and fight for your families, your sons and your daughters, your wives and your homes."

NEHEMIAH 4:7-9,13-14

G.K. Chesterton said, "The true soldier fights not because he hates what is in front of him, but because he loves what is behind him."

Men are made by God to be protectors and defenders.

It's not that we are to go out looking for a fight. But as men, you have to be ready to defend and protect those you love or the innocent victims of evil when the fight unavoidably comes to you.

This involves both spiritual action and, at times, when necessary, physical action.

We are to be men of prayer. This means we have a genuine relationship with God and we talk with Him and sincerely seek His protection in our lives and over our loved ones. Prayer is REAL. And the spiritual reality behind conflict in the lives of God's people is ultimately what is driving the conflict.

Are you actively praying for your wife and children? Do you initiate spiritual conversations, growth, and strength in your home? Do you know how to recognize the spiritual attacks that come against you and your family?

As important as it is, our responsibility as men doesn't end with prayer. We must also be men who are equipped and prepared to act in the natural realm, not just the supernatural realm. They are inextricably linked.

So we earnestly pray, and we post a guard. We stand ready to physically protect and defend others. We take the lead in confronting and neutralizing physical threats.

Those who serve in the military or in law enforcement are worthy of our respect and honor. They have chosen a profession and service that embodies a key part of the ethos of biblical manhood.

But even if you do not serve in this kind of profession, you must still be ready to jump in when called upon or when a situation arises. To use your God-given strength and masculinity to defend the helpless.

Men are indeed capable of violence and this is not always a bad thing.

Yes, men have abused their strength and there are evil men who act in sinfully violent ways. They are actually weak men. It takes good men, who exercise righteous violence, to stop weak and evil men who would abuse and hurt others.

Men need to pray against spiritual threats and men need to post guard against physical threats. Both are part of what it means to be a man.

WEEK NINE

We are living in a time not too dissimilar to Nehemiah's day. There are those seeking to persecute the Lord's servants and oppose the work of the Kingdom of God. And those who would prey on innocent people, like children in our schools and worshippers in a church gathering.

Sometimes the spiritual battle does, in fact, turn physical. Though our battle is not primarily or ultimately against flesh and blood, there are those who are used as tools of the enemy to inflict real harm on God's people, or helpless people.

What is a Christian man to do? **Pray to God and post a guard**. Pray and post. Pray and protect. Employ spiritual and physical measures.

For example, though a controversial topic in our day, it's okay to own weapons. Jesus said, "take a sword." He told Peter to put it away when Peter was misunderstanding God's will. But He didn't condemn the possession and use of a sword outright. Self-defense is biblical. Defense of the weak and vulnerable is biblical.

Stronger Men understand their role as a protector includes being ready, willing, and able to employ necessary strength and even violence to defend their life, family, property, and the weak and vulnerable.

It is not something we seek out. In many ways, it is something we seek to avoid. But there are times when an evil attack may come and we ought to be ready to meet the challenge and threat as men.

This is not a violation of the Bible's call for us to be peacemakers and men of peace. Nor is it a violation of Jesus' command to love our enemy or turn the other cheek.

Surely, wisdom is needed and each situation needs to be weighed carefully.

But it is not spiritual or godly to silently and passively stand by while innocent victims are killed or your wife and children are being physically threatened and harmed.

Sadly, but necessarily, churches need to have security teams ready to physically protect the flock from any who would seek to kill or do harm.

Your own family needs the same, and that's your job as a man.

Your neighbor who might be a single mom or an elderly couple may also need a protector one day...and it would be a noble thing for you, as a man, to rise to that threat, put yourself in harm's way, and protect those in need.

That's what a Stronger Man would do. Are you capable and prepared for that job?

There is a time to attempt to gently turn away wrath and to seek to live at peace with all men. And there are times where that isn't possible; therefore, there is also a time for violence.

WEEK NINE

Not reckless, vengeful, or sinful violence. Not taking justice into our own hands. But the holy use of strength for the noble protection of innocent, vulnerable people.

Men, you are built to protect. Spiritually, emotionally, relationally, and yes, physically. Prepare your minds now and get equipped to act with prayerful and physical courage when needed.

"Don't be afraid of them. Remember the Lord, who is great and awesome, and fight for your families, your sons and your daughters, your wives and your homes."

James A. Garfield—the 20th president and only ordained minister to become president—once said, "Of course I deprecate war, but if it is brought to my door the bringer will find me at home."

That's the way of a good soldier. That's the way of a Stronger Man.

LET'S PRAY

Lord, help me be ready, willing, and able to meet the needs of the hour both spiritually and physically as a protector of others. Help me be a man of peace, capable of righteous force, to defend the weak and vulnerable. Train my heart and hands for war, that I might honor You with my God-given masculine strength. Fill me with both compassion and courage. In Jesus' Name, amen.

SOLDIER

FROM A STRONGER MAN

My name is Justin. I'm 52 years old. I've been married to my beautiful bride for 28 years and we have two adult children. I'm a retired law enforcement officer. I've always been a "protector" at heart, so this career path was a natural fit. I worked in the jail for 4 ½ years, then a police officer for nearly 21 years, with 15 of those years serving as a SWAT Team member. I moved through the ranks and spent a few years as the Team Leader. I was also an instructor in several specialty disciplines. I was driven and focused on honing my skills as a "tactical soldier" in order to become the best physical "protector" I could be. I was willing to put my life on the line for others. I've successfully faced countless high stress encounters in my career. Partly due to my training. Partly due to the team members I had with me. But this was all at a cost—between constant training and call-outs, I was not home and I missed more family events than I care to mention.

There was another cost to this—a greater cost. Behind the scenes of being a successful "tactical soldier," I was losing the spiritual battle. I was under the curse of pridefulness and selfishness, and I was a slave to pornography. I kept it hidden and avoided any type of accountability. It caused me to drift further and further away from my bride and to be short-tempered with my son. I could see it, and I could feel it. Every time I went down that sinful path of destruction, I'd get a gut-wrenching knot in my stomach. Yet, I continued. I allowed Satan to convince me that what I was doing was not as bad as what others have done. I bought into his lie and allowed myself to justify my sins, by comparing them to the sins of others.

I finally hit a breaking point. I was exhausted from this self-centered way of life. I kept trying to convince myself I had this all under control. Then I realized the truth—the sins in my life had control of me. While attending Easter service in 2017, I heard Jesus say, "Follow me." Unbelievably, I still fought against it. It didn't make sense. I wouldn't hesitate to run towards gunfire, yet I was scared to let go of "self." But Jesus was lovingly persistent and kept calling to me. I knew it was time. I decided to accept Jesus as my Lord and Savior, and I got baptized that very day!

My life has not been the same since! Jesus took away all of my fleshly desires and set me free from the bondage of pornography. Jesus has also transformed my heart. I finally figured out that I couldn't fight against spiritual warfare alone. I needed Jesus to help protect my heart and to give me the strength I need to be a successful "soldier" in the battle of spiritual warfare. I desired, and knew I needed, a new training regiment and new tactics in order to be better equipped for this battle. Because I quickly learned that salvation does not stop demonic attacks—those actually increase. So I built a new "tactical team" of godly men to surround myself with. I learned new "strategic maneuvers" by actively seeking out their wisdom and wise counsel. I began studying a new "play book" with daily Bible reading. And I conducted new "debriefs" by insisting on accountability.

Now I'm able to recognize these attacks when they come, and I'm equipped with the power of the Holy Spirit to fight them off. Spiritual warfare is never-ending, friends. And it will happen when you least expect it. That's one of Satan's tactics, to catch you when your guard is down. This is why I choose to live every day in "biblical saturation." What I listen to, what I watch, what I read, who I surround myself with…it all matters!

I have also learned how to truly and intentionally lead my bride and my household. And I've seen the resulting fruit from this. My bride is thriving, because she knows I am absolutely committed to her and our marriage. My children have drawn closer to me, because they now have a godly example of what a humble, but loving father looks like. This is why I strive to be a godly man—a Stronger Man.

Justin, 52

SOLDIER

REFLECT & DISCUSS

1. What are your thoughts and feelings about being a spiritual and physical protector?

2. Have you ever had to use physical strength or force to defend or protect yourself or someone else?

3. When do you believe physical force/response is godly?

4. In what ways do you need to prepare better for your role as a protector?

5. Of the two realms, spiritual and physical, which one are you currently more equipped in? How would you get stronger in the other? Who do you know who could help you?

___

6. What are ways a Stronger Man should spiritually protect his family?

___

7. What's your next step to be more prepared and equipped to spiritually protect? Physically protect?

___

TAKE ACTION

- What are the key elements necessary to spiritually and physically protect your family? Write out a plan of what that looks like in your situation. Begin to implement that plan this week, month, or quarter.

WEEK 10

THE WORLD IS NOT WORTHY

And what more shall I say? I do not have time to tell about Gideon, Barak, Samson and Jephthah, about David and Samuel and the prophets, who through faith conquered kingdoms, administered justice, and gained what was promised; who shut the mouths of lions, quenched the fury of the flames, and escaped the edge of the sword; **whose weakness was turned to strength**; and who became powerful in battle and routed foreign armies. Women received back their dead, raised to life again. There were others who were tortured, refusing to be released so that they might gain an even better resurrection. Some faced jeers and flogging, and even chains and imprisonment. They were put to death by stoning; they were sawed in two; they were killed by the sword. They went about in sheepskins and goatskins, destitute, persecuted and mistreated… **the world was not worthy of them**. They wandered in deserts and mountains, living in caves and in holes in the ground.

HEBREWS 11:32-38

If that's not a list of good soldiering I don't know what is.

Gideon, Barak, Samson, Jephthah, David, Samuel, the prophets.

The beginning of Hebrews chapter 11 tells us, "*Now faith is being sure of what we hope for and certain of what we do not see. THIS is what the ancients were commended for.*"

What is it that made them Stronger Men and makes us Stronger Men? One straightforward way to answer that question is the biblical word "faith."

"By faith...By faith...By faith..." Hebrews 11, the "Hall of Faith" chapter of the Bible, recounts the great Old Testament heroes of the faith. Men (and women) like Abel, Enoch, Noah, Abraham, Isaac, Jacob, Joseph, Moses (and even his parents), the Israelites, and Rahab.

And then we get to this paragraph of the honorable mentions! Which is just jaw-dropping.

If you don't know the stories of these characters, take the time to go back and read the accounts of their lives.

WEEK TEN

All of them were flawed characters, yet God still chose to save them and empower them and use them. The difference was their courageous moments and actions fueled by faith. Rusty as it often was.

FAITH in God and in His promise enabled them to do great and mighty things.

They conquered kingdoms. Administered justice. Shut the mouths of lions. Quenched the fury of the flames. Escaped the edge of the sword. Their weakness was turned to strength. They became powerful in battle. They routed foreign armies. That's man stuff.

It reads like a running list of epic cinematic blockbusters.

FAITH also enabled them to do good and noble things.

Like bless and protect and deliver women and children. Stronger Men fight for the freedom of others. Man stuff.

FAITH enabled them to endure great hardship and suffering.

Torture. Conviction—refusing to be released. Jeers. Flogging. Chains. Imprisonment. Destitute. Persecuted. Mistreated. Wandered in deserts and mountains. Lived in caves and holes in the ground. Man stuff.

FAITH enabled them not just to live for great and noble things, not just to endure difficult suffering, but even to die well, with faith and honor intact.

Stoned. Sawed in two. Killed by the sword. Man stuff.

But the greatest thing that could be said about these heroes of the faith:

The world was not worthy of them.

Let us give honor where honor is due. Well done, good and faithful servants.

Faith will enable you to follow in their steps.

And above all these incredible examples, just a few verses later the author of Hebrews tells us, *"Let us fix our eyes on Jesus, the author and perfecter of our faith, who for the joy set before Him endured the cross, scorning its shame, and sat down at the right hand of the throne of God. Consider Him who endured such opposition from sinful men, so that you will not grow weary and lose heart"* (**Hebrews 12:2-3**).

Do not grow weary! Do not lose heart! You were made for greatness.

Made to live your life as another scene and chapter of world-changing courage in God's incredible Epic Story of Faith.

Every generation has men who step up as heroes of the faith.

Just because the Bible is done being written does not mean the mission of God is done producing these kind of men. Not all will be written into a book or recorded in history. But God knows each one. They are men like you and me who are fixing their eyes on Jesus, surrounded by His incredible army of witnesses who have gone before.

You were created and called to join their ranks.

David served God's purpose in his own generation. And then died (Acts 13:36). You may not be David, but you're called to do the same.

WEEK TEN

How will you serve the purposes of God in your own generation?

How will faith propel you to live into the greatness of God's call on your life?

This world needs faithful men, faithful husbands, faithful dads, faithful sons, faithful pastors, church planters, business owners, workers, builders, leaders, servants, doctors, lawyers, teachers, engineers, bankers, techies, innovators, communicators, designers, musicians, storytellers, governors, mayors, cops, and yes, soldiers.

By faith, be one of those men.

LET'S PRAY

Lord, thank You for the great men that have gone before me. Thank You above them all for the greatest example, the greatest Man, Jesus Christ. Teach me to follow in His footsteps, as other men of faith have. Help me rise to the challenge and needs of my generation and live for Your purposes as a man of faith. Come what may, help me fix my eyes on You and not lose heart. In Jesus' Name, amen.

SOLDIER

Soldier is a role that is easy for me to identify with. While I never served in the armed forces, I have worked in law enforcement for nearly 20 years. A profession where self-sacrifice and protecting others is an everyday occurrence. However, 2021 had me and many other law enforcement officers really wondering if we had chosen the right path. Over time, I began to realize that every time I got discouraged and thought about doing something different, I felt empty. I felt empty because I had not chosen my path, God chose it for me. He called me to be a police officer, and He has placed me exactly where he needs me to be.

Similarly, God has also called me to be a husband, father, friend, and son. He chose all those paths too. Each of these roles comes with opportunities to protect, lead, guide, and love those around me. As a husband. I need to protect my own heart and mind from sin so I can protect my marriage and protect my wife. As a father, I need to set a good example for my son and daughter, so they can see what being a godly man looks like—for my son, so he can become one, and for my daughter, so she can find one. I want to be the friend my friends turn to when they are in need. And as a son, I want to follow my heavenly Father's lead. **Daily, I have to work at staying focused on God** and fulfilling my many roles as God would want me to do. Thankfully, God has surrounded me with men who are good husbands, good fathers, good friends, and most importantly, strong Christian men who call themselves sons of the Most High.

It is these men who make up the army I am in. These are the soldiers who I fight alongside protecting God's design, God's plan for the Church, our country, our community, our families, and our friends. These are the Stronger Men I choose to surround myself with, and we are all pursuing THE Stronger Man together.

Brian, 43

> "War must be, while we defend our lives against a destroyer who would devour all; but I do not love the bright sword for its sharpness, nor the arrow for its swiftness, nor the warrior for his glory. I love only that which they defend."
>
> — J.R.R. Tolkien, The Lord of the Rings: The Two Towers

SOLDIER

REFLECT & DISCUSS

1. What do you hope others say about you when you're dead and gone?

_____
_____
_____

2. How can you prepare now to be strong if and when faced with persecution and suffering for your faith?

_____
_____
_____

3. What is God calling you to do with the rest of your life? How would you write it in a sentence?

_____
_____
_____

4. What battles and challenges are you facing this week?

_____
_____
_____

WEEK TEN

5. What would it look like for you to face those challenges by faith?

___

6. What is the most difficult thing you've had to face or endure for your faith?

___

7. Faith is most clearly seen in action, in obedience to God's command. Where do you currently need greater obedience?

___

TAKE ACTION

- Memorize Hebrews 11:1.

- This week, make note of anything that you do, or endure, simply or purely because of your faith. Write them down. Reflect on the role faith plays in your daily actions and attitudes.

- Write down at least one hard thing that you need to do this week in obedience to the Lord. By faith, follow through and obey in that area.

WEEK 11

STRONGER MEN MAKE STRONGER MEN

Then Jesus came to them and said, "All authority in Heaven and on earth has been given to me. Therefore go and

MAKE DISCIPLES

of all nations, baptizing them in the name of the Father and of the Son and of the Holy Spirit, and teaching them to obey everything I have commanded you. And surely I am with you always, to the very end of the age."

MATTHEW 28:18-20

Stronger Men follow Jesus, the true Stronger Man.

Which means they become like Jesus. And part of becoming like Jesus is building up other men to become like Jesus.

Disciples make disciples. Who make disciples.

Stronger Men build Stronger Men. Who build Stronger Men.

The great mission Jesus gave to His disciples is found in various forms in the gospels. The most well known is in Matthew 28.

After dying on the cross for our sin, Jesus rose again on the third day. He holds the keys to death and Hell. He has all power and authority. Nothing and no one can stop His advancing mission. Not even death itself.

The declaration of the early church was, "Jesus is Lord." In other words, He is our commanding officer.

When He says, "Go," we go. When He says, "Make," we make. When He says, "Baptize," we baptize. When He says, "Teach," we teach.

Copy that.

It isn't just for pastors. It's for all Christians, all followers of Jesus, all disciples. All men.

It's called the Great Commission. It's not the Great Suggestion.

So, men, we've got to figure it out. It's our mission.

The good news is, Jesus also promised that we're not alone. Furthermore, He doesn't send us out in our own power or authority. He sends us out with His all-encompassing authority and in the power of His Spirit.

We are sent by the King. He has the authority to commission and send us as His ambassadors. We now have a delegated authority to carry out that mission.

Thankfully, we can see in the lives of those disciples who heard that command, a pretty clear picture of what that looks like in action. We can see what Jesus did with them in the gospels and then we can see what they did after He gave them this commission in the book of Acts.

There is one main, central, imperative command in the Matthew 28 commission: *"Make disciples."*

If we are called to make disciples, we better know what one is. In its simplest terms, a disciple is a student, learner, or follower.

It is one who takes on the beliefs and practices of another. Someone who disciplines themselves to become like their teacher. Both inwardly and outwardly. The motivations and desires, and the actions and lifestyle.

> **We are called to become like Jesus. To love what He loves. To love how He loves. To be about what He is about. To serve how He served. And to tell others what He has told us.**

A disciple of Jesus is someone who is increasingly orienting their life around the person of Jesus, loving Him, trusting Him, and submitting to His lordship in every area of life.

Suffice it to say, gentlemen, this isn't a weekend project. It's a lifelong endeavor. It requires a serious commitment and a purposeful devotion.

If you're not a little bit intimidated, uncertain, or sober-minded, you're probably not paying attention, or have never actually tried to disciple someone. And if you are some mix of those things, congratulations and welcome to the club.

But that's no excuse to keep us from engaging in the task.

Jesus will take you as you are, where you are, and start to train you for the work. It starts with you, your family, your neighbors, those closest to you and goes on from there. But remember, you can't export what you don't have.

How do you make disciples? Here are three big ideas to get started:

1 THERE'S A CALL TO FOLLOW.

Jesus said, "Follow me. And I will make you fishers of men."

It starts with a vision of who God wants us to become and an invitation to others into a relationship to intentionally move in that direction.

If they aren't interested in it, it's going to be tougher. It takes intentionality on your part and the work of the Spirit in their heart.

In your own house and family, you bring them along with you. Beyond the walls of your home, you're looking for the near and the hungry. Someone who is leaning in or open to considering pursuing Jesus and what it would mean for them to become a Stronger Man.

Making disciples and building Stronger Men starts by walking with others in the direction Jesus wants them to go. So you start by building a relationship. Learn where they've come from and where they're going. What motivates them and what holds them back? Where do they find their identity and what's their understanding of the purpose for their life? Along the way, you begin to share about how Jesus has changed your life. And what Jesus is up to in the world through the unfolding story of God as you engage with the story of the Bible.

2. THERE'S A CALL TO DIE TO SELF. To grow and change.

As we follow Jesus, there are things that have to fall away. Some things need to change. Jesus has a way of exposing our hearts and challenging us at the core, revealing who and what we love, worship, and follow.

At some point, we wrestle with the big questions and have to answer, "*Who do you say that I am?*" Somewhere along the way, we come to a crisis of belief or faith...and we decide if we believe Jesus really is who He said He is. Is He the Son of God and the Savior of sinners? Is He my Savior? Is He the Lord? Is He my Lord? Is He worthy of worship and surrender?

Jesus said, "*No one can be my disciple unless he denies himself, picks up his cross daily, and follows me.*" And this process of testing and refining our devotion to Jesus is a lifelong process and pursuit of growth and change. Where we continually and increasingly yield every part of our life to the Lordship of Jesus.

3. And then, eventually, THERE'S A CALL TO LEAD OTHERS.

I do, you watch. I do, you help. You do, I help. You do, someone else watches.

"*What you've seen and heard in me, pass on to others.*"

Where are you in the discipleship journey? Is it your turn to step up and lead others while still being coached and equipped along the way?

Grab some men. Get in their life. Get to know them. Take an interest. Serve them. Invite them into your life. Show them the impact Jesus has made in your life. Ask them questions. Welcome them into your home. Share some meals. Do some fun activities together. Orient conversations around the things of God; purpose, meaning, identity, truth, character, and biblical manhood.

Introduce them to other godly men in your life. Pray for the Spirit to move in their life. Help them start to read the Bible. Share and show how the Word of God is changing your life. Teach them to pray. Model it and challenge them to start.

Be available to answer their questions or point them in the direction of more good content. Don't be afraid to challenge them in areas where you see blind spots or weaknesses, but do it with love and faith for them. Show how the truth of God impacts their marriage, parenting, vocation, money, time, priorities, attitude, and response to trials. Give them opportunities to share what they're learning and give them responsibility to share in serving others.

Do you see what's happening? You're well on your way in discipling them to disciple others.

And here's the kicker...you won't actually become a Stronger Man yourself until you're intentionally seeking to build Stronger Men yourself. One of the ways we become stronger is by engaging in the work of helping build others.

You really only need to be one step ahead to start helping someone else take their first steps.

Let us encourage one another, spur one another on, and build each other up as we go and make disciples.

This is the way of a good soldier. Leaning into the mission. Making disciples. This is the way of a Stronger Man.

LET'S PRAY

Lord, use me to lead other men to You. I want to be a builder of men. I want to obey Your command to make disciples of others. Help me start in my own home, in my family. Give me wisdom and courage to prioritize the disciple-making mission of Jesus with my time, energy, resources, and influence. In Jesus' Name, amen.

WEEK ELEVEN

SOLDIER

FROM A STRONGER MAN

I walked into Grace City Church nearly a year ago. Until then, I had lived a life full of sin. I had a lot of deep wounds in my past. And the world sold me a false sense of manhood and how to deal with the pain. The sin grew worse and the wounds deeper.

But God had other plans. I will never forget the night—being completely alone, terrified of the evil I found myself faced with. I slammed my eyes shut and cried out, "God, I need you now!" I am still amazed that God rescued me right then. I didn't deserve it; I had done terrible things in my past.

From that moment, the healing began. I had been walking through the valley of death, drowning in my sin. That's when Jesus launched my rescue mission. As each snare was cut away, my love for Jesus grew deeper.

As Jesus began to change my life, I remember moments of being afraid. Afraid of losing the old way of life, old friends, old habits, and my identity of who and what the world said I was. The tough guy I made myself out to be. But God had a plan for me. He surrounded me with new men—men from Grace City. Suddenly, I had new friends, new brothers, and a new way of life. The men that God has surrounded me with are of the absolute highest caliber. Men I have relied upon in the trenches. When the going got tough, they didn't back down. Men who rallied around me and were committed to guarding me. **The Lord continued by taking away my old desires and giving me new ones. Most importantly, He showed me my true identity in Jesus Christ.**

Where I was lowly and wretched, Jesus now makes me stand upright. Where I was immoral and unjust, Jesus makes me righteous. Where I was broken, He has healed my wounds. Where I was afraid, He fills me with courage. When I was in danger, He rescued me. When I was a sinner He loved me. He showed me grace. He died for me.

WEEK ELEVEN

I no longer care for the standards of this world. I long to live for the Lord. I want to know Him more, to follow and obey Him. Without Jesus, I am nothing. But with Him, I have the courage to stand firm and push back against the very chains that once held me captive—to stand among the ranks of the Saints marching forward.

Today, I'm digging in. I help lead other men out of bondage. I am honored to walk beside them through the battle. I do this because I love Jesus, who saved my soul from death. He calls me to do better, to do more, to fight the good fight—to be a Stronger Man.

Jake, 36

REFLECT & DISCUSS

1. Who has had the biggest impact on you spiritually?

2. How did they relate to you and impact you?

3. What was it about them that impacted you most?

4. Who is in your life that you could begin praying for and looking for opportunities to invite into this kind of journey?

WEEK ELEVEN

5. Where in your life do you need to die to self? In what ways do you need to grow and change over the next year?

_____
_____
_____

6. What would it look like for you to take the next step to grow as a follower of Jesus? What do you think might be able to accelerate that growth?

_____
_____
_____

7. If you made disciple-making, Stronger Men-building a serious priority for the next 10, 15, 20 years...what could happen? In your family? In your circle of influence?

_____
_____
_____

TAKE ACTION

- Send a note of thanks this week to those who have discipled and positively impacted your journey of faith with Jesus.

- Make a list of men you think the Lord is putting on your heart to disciple. Begin praying for them. Send them a text to encourage them. Consider inviting them to go back through this book with you in the near future.

WEEK 12

THE STRONGER MAN WILL FINISH THE WAR

I saw Heaven standing open and there before me was a white horse, whose rider is called Faithful and True. With justice He judges and wages war. His eyes are like blazing fire, and on His head are many crowns. He has a Name written on Him that no one knows but He Himself. He is dressed in a robe dipped in blood, and His Name is the Word of God. The armies of Heaven were following Him, riding on white horses and dressed in fine linen, white and clean. Coming out of His mouth is a sharp sword with which to strike down the nations. He will rule them with an iron scepter. He treads the winepress of the fury of the wrath of God Almighty. On His robe and on His thigh He has this Name written:

KING OF KINGS & LORD OF LORDS.

REVELATION 19:11-16

One day, the war will end.

The final battle will be won and we will have rest on all sides.

What a day of rejoicing and victory that will be! For the wicked and sinful, it will be a terrible day of judgment and wrath. But for the righteous and redeemed, it will be a glorious day of salvation.

Until that day comes, or until we die...the war will rage on and the fight must be fought.

But when that day comes, swords will finally be put away, beat into plowshares, and spears turned into pruning hooks.

The hope of future final victory and the return of our great God and Savior is a source of great strength and encouragement for followers of Jesus. For good soldiers and Stronger Men.

On the days when we are tempted to give up, give in, or quit...we must remember that victory has been secured and that none of our fighting is ever in vain.

When you're weary, imagine that day. When you're the target of a malicious attack, imagine that day.

Every wrong will be made right. Every disease healed. Every tear wiped away. Every evil man laid low. Every injustice undone. Every wrong sentence made right. True justice delivered. Perfect, holy, and righteous.

You'll take a seat. Take off your boots. Drop your shield. And be greeted with the most beautiful sound you've ever heard: *"Well done, good and faithful servant. Enter into your Master's joy."*

Your faith will now be sight. You'll see your Savior face-to-face. The scars of the nail pierced hands and feet, and the sword-pierced side of your battle-worn resurrected King will be at your fingertips.

The cloud of witnesses will be cheering. The angels will be worshipping. You'll cross the finish line and walk into the great celestial city. The gates will be open. The streets will be gold. The table will be set. The party will commence. Every sore muscle and aging joint will be rejuvenated. Your strength will be renewed like in the days of your youth. The feast will be spectacular. The joy will be palpable.

The great scenes in the movies can help but still can't do it justice. It will be greater still than anything you've ever imagined.

You'll be welcomed into the presence of God in all His glory and holiness and majesty. You'll fall to your knees in worship. The roar of

WEEK TWELVE

worship will resound like crashing waves. The crown that was placed on your head as you received your reward, you will lay down at His feet in humble adoration.

The reunions will be so sweet.

The stories around the fireside will be riveting. The laughter will be explosive. The "ohs" and "ahs" will repeat.

The ones you've read of and heard of will be there: Abraham, Moses, Joshua, David, Isaiah, Samuel, Mary, Peter, Paul, John.

Not just those in the Bible but throughout history. Martin Luther, George Whitefield, Charles Spurgeon, Jonathan Edwards, William Tyndale, John Bunyan, William Carey, C.S. Lewis, Billy Graham.

Just as amazing will be meeting the ones you've yet to know their name. The untold stories of martyrs and preachers and unsung heroes of the faith through the ages.

It will never get dull, never get old, never be boring. There'll be endless opportunities for adventure and activity without the weight of the curse and without the presence of sin, Satan, and evil.

And greatest of all will be the presence of the Father and Jesus the Son and the Spirit of God. In the center. Giving it all life and light. Walking with us again in the cool of the day. Alongside the River of Life.

Eternal rest. Eternal bliss. Eternal life.

And it will all be worth it. Every sin confessed. Every prayer prayed. Every tear shed. Every battle fought.

So brothers, do not give up. Remember that day that is coming.

The sun will rise—the great morning star, whose rays bring healing and whose light shines brighter until the full light of day—and bring warmth that will never again grow cold. Lift your face and feel the warm, golden beams. As surely as the sun rises, He will appear. Bolster your courage another day and strengthen the brothers around you. Stand your ground and fight to protect those under your care. Lay down your life and lift up the Name above every name. He is Lord. He is King. He is the Great Warrior. The Rider on the White Horse and the battle is His.

Recall the scene at the end of the Lord of the Rings: The Two Towers... "Sam's Speech." (If you haven't seen the Lord of the Rings, the challenge has been issued.) It goes like this...

Frodo: (exhausted & weary) I can't do this, Sam...

Sam: (weary but resolved and with conviction) I know! It's all wrong!
By rights we shouldn't even be here.
But we are.
It's like in the great stories Mr. Frodo.
The ones that really mattered.
Full of darkness and danger they were,
and sometimes you didn't want to know the end.
Because how could the end be happy.
How could the world go back to the way it was when so much bad happened.
But in the end, it's only a passing thing, this shadow.
Even darkness must pass.
A new day will come.
And when the sun shines it will shine out the clearer.
Those were the stories that stayed with you.
That meant something.
Even if you were too small to understand why.

But I think, Mr. Frodo, I do understand.
I know now.
Folk in those stories had lots of chances of turning back only they didn't.
Because they were holding on to something.

Frodo: What are we holding on to, Sam?

Sam: That there's some good in this world, Mr. Frodo. And it's worth fighting for.

"To Him who is able to keep you from stumbling and to present you before His glorious presence without fault and with great joy—to the only God our Savior be glory, majesty, power and authority, through Jesus Christ our Lord, before all ages, now and forevermore! Amen."
Jude 24-25

That's the hope of a good soldier. The hope of a Stronger Man. Carry it with you today.

LET'S PRAY

Lord, what a vision of Heaven! What a picture of eternal life to come! Thank You for going to prepare a place for us, for me. Encourage my heart when I'm tempted to despair. Keep this vision, this future reality, before my eyes today. That it's worth it to live for You, to stay in the fight, to resist the enemy, and to lay down my life in the service of King Jesus. Fill me and strengthen me today, and use me to encourage others. In Jesus' Name, amen.

SOLDIER

FROM A STRONGER MAN

I always wanted to be a soldier. I played "Army" as a kid all the time. Both my grandfathers served in the military. My father died when I was an infant, but my mom always told me about his service to this great country in Vietnam as a United States Marine. My stepfather served in the Army National Guard as a medic. I knew from a very early age I would be in the military.

I signed up for the United States Army while a junior in high school. I signed up for the Infantry. I could not think of a more cool thing than being a Soldier. I graduated high school and off I went to basic training at Fort Benning in Georgia.

I graduated from boot camp and AIT (Advanced Individual Training) and was stationed with the 24th Infantry Division at Fort Stewart in Georgia. I was deployed to Iraq during Desert Shield/ Desert Storm. I earned the coveted Combat Infantry Badge (CIB). I was living the dream.

I left the Army to attend school, work, and get back to being a civilian. I married my best friend, and we had two amazing children. One girl and one boy. I was hired to be another form of Soldier—a Deputy Sheriff. Life was so good.

While at the Basic Law Enforcement Academy in Burien, WA I received a phone call from my bride that shook me to the core. She hated to let me know via phone, but she had to tell me right away. She had been having some health issues and had been seeing doctors and having tests done. My bride called to tell me she had been diagnosed with Multiple Sclerosis (MS). I have heard the expression several times in my life, "It was like a gut punch." This was no gut punch. I felt like I had been run over by a train.

Two babies...my bride is going to die...I'm working shift work as a Deputy Sheriff...guilt I was not there (in person) to comfort my bride. My mind was going a million miles per hour, in all directions. A short time later, my then five-year-old son was diagnosed with depression. The doctor believed it was from me being gone all week to attend the academy for months on end. I again was not there for my son. Being run over by yet another train in such a short time period absolutely rocked my world.

I know this sounds odd, but being run over by those two trains changed my life for the better.

My bride and I got educated more about MS. I now knew she would not die…well, at least in the near future. I returned home from the academy, and was out doing my dream job at night. My son was healed from his depression because he could now hang out with his dad every day again.

My bride and I pursued God together for the first time. Our marriage was good. God made it even better! God made me and my bride better parents to our two children. We both agreed we would not let the fire we feel for God go out. **I don't want to be a spark for God…I want to be a bonfire for God.** I then, now, and forever want to be a Soldier for my Father. God saved me by grace and grace alone. I did not earn it. Those two trains running me over lit a fire under this Soldier that will never be extinguished!

Brandon, 52

REFLECT & DISCUSS

1. How often do you think of Heaven?

2. What kind of thoughts and feelings does thinking and talking about "the end" bring up? Why do you think that is?

3. What most encourages you or excites you as you think of it today?

4. What questions do you have about what Heaven will be like?

WEEK TWELVE

5. In addition to Jesus Himself, what other biblical or historical Christian are you most excited to meet & why?

_____

_____

_____

6. When are you most tempted to "give up"? What and/or who has God used to "keep you going?

_____

_____

_____

7. Why is it important that we contemplate Heaven and think about eternity often?

_____

_____

_____

TAKE ACTION

- If you could write your own epitaph, a short description on your gravestone, what would you want it to say? Write it this week. Share it with your wife and family. Give them the same assignment. Ask them what they would want theirs to be. What adjustments do you need to make as a family for that epitaph to be true before you die or before Christ returns?

- Find 3 additional passages in the Bible that speak about the hope and glory of Jesus returning. Write them down. What are the common themes in those passages?

ADDITIONAL QUESTIONS FOR DISCUSSION

1. What's the hardest thing you've ever done in life?

2. What's a fear you've experienced that you've had to overcome? How did you overcome it?

3. Have you ever been in a fight? How would you describe that experience? Was it necessary or unnecessary? Looking back, what would you do differently?

4. When is fighting (using physical force) necessary or even noble?

5. How should men pursue being peacemakers? What can you attempt to do to diffuse situations from escalating to violence?

6. What is your favorite outdoor physical activity or hobby?

7. If you could be any animal, what would it be and why?

8. How do you plan to stay physically fit as you get older so that you can continue to be ready to use your physical strength to serve and protect those around you?

9. What goes into being a spiritual protector of your family? What should you be on the lookout for?

10. Who is your favorite action movie hero/figure and why?

11. Who is your favorite historical leader/figure (other than Jesus) and why?

12. What is the craziest experience you've had with the forces of nature? (water, fire, wind, weather, etc.)

13. What is the wildest experience you've had with wildlife?

14. What/when is the most scared you've been in your life? How did you react/respond in that situation?

15. What is the worst job you've ever had? Why was it the worst?

16. What is the best job you've ever had? Why was it the best?

17. Which branch of the military is your favorite? Why?

18. Who is the best example you personally know of a Stronger Man fulfilling the role of Soldier/protector?

19. When you think of someone you know who has endured suffering well, and is a good example of perseverance, who comes to mind?

20. Where do you see yourself in 5 years? 10 years? How is life different? How are you different? What will it take to end up there?

PRACTICAL WAYS TO LEAN INTO BEING A SOLDIER, BUILT TO PROTECT

- Be prepared to physically, spiritually, and emotionally protect your family.
- Regularly scan your environment for potential threats.
- Become comfortable and proficient with specific weapons of your choice.
- Lock up the house at night. Secure the premises anywhere your family is staying.
- Be the one to investigate loud noises or suspicious situations.
- Cultivate and use your physical strength and ability to fix and repair broken things around the house.
- Carry any heavy items for your wife/mom/sister.
- Unload the groceries from the car.
- Be the one to get out of the car and fill it with gas at gas stations.
- Walk on the traffic side of any sidewalk or roadway.
- Do the bulk of the driving, especially in stressful conditions, heavy traffic, or inclement weather.
- Take care of routine auto maintenance.
- Regularly open doors. Be the last one to enter the building. Be the first one to exit, holding the door from the outside while scanning your environment.
- Be the last one getting on a bus, train, elevator, or escalator.
- Sit strategically in restaurants and public places so you can quickly see any threats and be in a position to engage the threat from a place of tactical advantage.
- Sign up for any school, church, or other security role opportunities where your family is involved.
- Be the one to answer the door at home, especially if it is an unknown visitor.
- Take the lead in interacting with any strangers.

- If someone contacts your wife or family, put yourself closest to them and be prepared to intervene in the conversation. Be ready to take the lead.
- After scanning the environment, walk up to any counter with your wife at hotels, car rental services, banks, and any other establishments that might be stressful for your wife or where people might try to take advantage of a woman.
- Take the lead in any family or relational conflict situations.
- Initiate taking your family to church.
- Initiate prayer and Bible reading.
- Ask questions about your family's day. Truly listen.
- Ask questions and facilitate discussion about movies or shows watched in your home. Check a site like PluggedIn to review content of any movies.
- Be aware of the music your kids are listening to. Ensure the content is appropriate.
- Take the lead on managing technology usage in the home and applying safety measures for when, what, where, and how screens are used and viewed. Employ accountability software.
- Discuss current events in the culture with your wife and kids. What are they thinking and believing about the situation? Does their thinking and response line up with biblical principles?
- To protect your wife and children emotionally, show them proper affection by giving hugs, making eye contact, saying "I love you," and expressing specific and personal affirmation of the qualities and characteristics you appreciate about them.
- Make sure you are dealing with any and all ungodly anger or ungodly attitudes in your own heart on a regular basis.
- Reject all forms and expressions of passivity.

THE STRONGER MAN CREED
by Josh McPherson

I am a **SOLDIER**.
With a King to serve and a battle to fight,
I will not go quiet into the night
or let my heart be filled with fright.
For all that's good and all that's right,
I make good battle with all my might.
I am courage in human form.
I am a vigilant Protector.

I am a **FARMER**.
Working a field to harvest a crop,
no matter the challenge, I will not stop.
Wherever I go, things flourish around
and come up from underneath the ground,
because I diligently water and sow
and care for things so that they grow.
I get it done. I do what it takes.
I am perseverance personified.
I am a diligent Provider.

I am an **ATHLETE**.
Running the race to win the crown,
no strain or pain will keep me down.
And one day I will hear the sound,
"Well done, good and faithful one."
That alone is why I run.
So I push hard to the very end.
I am a visionary Leader.

I am a **SON**.
Known and loved, I'm a man who's free
from a life of sin and misery
and self-imposed slavery.
Thanks to Jesus' work on Calvary,
I'm a blood-bought branch of the family tree!
Yes, I sing, Jesus loves even me!
Glory to the King of kings.
I am a lover of the one true God.

"Evil will win, good men are all gone,"
I often hear it said.
So lend me your ear, and let me be clear,
valor is not dead.

This is my pledge, my life, my code:
I will walk the narrow road.
Pushing, striving, sweating, straining,
hustling, growing, never caving
to the siren song of the me-centered life
I live for One, no matter the strife
That comes when fighting for good.

And with all my strength, I'll answer the bell
and hit with force the gates of hell.
This Soldier, Farmer, Athlete, Son
won't flinch in the storm, no matter what comes.
No matter what arrows the snake may hurl,
I'll Kill the Dragon, I'll Win the Girl.

I'll make good use of all my days
by spending them to proudly say,
I count myself among the clan
of those who follow the Stronger Man.

So that is what my life will proclaim.
With all I am, **All in, One Name!**

> "Aye, fight and you may die. Run, and you'll live...at least a while. And dying in your beds, many years from now, would you be willing to trade all the days, from this day to that, for one chance, just one chance, to come back here and tell our enemies that they may take our lives, but they'll never take... OUR FREEDOM!"
>
> — William Wallace, *Braveheart*

www.ingramcontent.com/pod-product-compliance
Lightning Source LLC
Chambersburg PA
CBHW071118090426
42736CB00012B/1945